A selection of the

Best Hotels & Res
in the Eastern Counties

Compiled by: Michael Campbell
Jane Costin

Edited by: James Lawrence

CONTENTS

Published by
Bracken Publishing
Bracken House, 199a Holt Road
Cromer, Norfolk NR27 9JN

ISBN 1 871614 07 4

Printed by Broadgate Printers, Aylsham, Norfolk.

August 1991

Foreword

As I sit watching Wimbledon on television, I realise how the weather has so drastically affected the fortnight's programme; but life goes on, all the matches will finish, all the strawberries will be eaten, and afterwards we will realise that even when nothing goes to plan, Wimbledon will have been yet another success.

Life is not easy for hoteliers and restaurateurs at the moment, but I would like to think that the moral from Wimbledon is that we must all smile through it, give ever better service, work harder to raise standards and value for money. Life is all about competition, and we must hope that a better financial climate is just around the corner.

As a former international rugby player, I have been privileged to travel a great deal, and dine in many a fine restaurant (not always appreciated at the time). Now on the other side of the bar, as it were, I, wife Jenny and staff strive to generate a happy, friendly atmosphere, good and varied food and, just as important, to have fun ourselves!

Dickie Jeeps, CBE.

Dickie is a former England rugby captain, and is co-proprietor (with wife Jenny) of Stocks Restaurant, Bottisham, near Cambridge (see page 35).

Important

Please note:–

1. *Dishes listed are examples only. Menus change frequently, so they will not necessarily be available at all times.*

2. *Prices, where quoted, may change during the currency of this guide. Average a la carte prices are based on a three course meal without wine.*

3. *Every effort is made to ensure accuracy, but inevitably circumstances alter and errors and omissions may occur. Therefore the publisher cannot accept liability for any consequences arising therefrom.*

4. *Your comments regarding establishments, whether featured or not, are especially welcome. All letters will be gratefully acknowledged, and correspondents who particularly impress will receive a free copy of the next edition.*

5. *This is a selection: it is not claimed that all the best hotels and restaurants in the region are featured.*

6. *A note to proprietors: if your establishment is not featured, please do not be offended! The area covered is very large, and time limited. If you serve good food in pleasant surrounds, and would like to be considered for the next edition, please write and let us know.*

FURTHER COPIES OF THIS OR OUR OTHER GUIDES MAY BE OBTAINED BY WRITING TO:

Bracken Publishing
Bracken House
199a Holt Road
Cromer
Norfolk NR27 9JN

Other guides:

Best Inns & Pubs in the Eastern Counties
Best Inns & Pubs in the Cotswolds, Thames Valley & Chilterns
Best Inns & Pubs in the Midlands
Best Inns & Pubs in the West Country
Best Inns & Pubs in the South East

Enclose payment of £3.50 per book, to include postage and packing.

No order will be accepted without prior payment, other than from recognised book retailers.

Young Restaurateur of the Year

Steven Saunders, proprietor (with wife Sally) of the celebrated Pink Geranium at Melbourn in Cambridgeshire, is the recent recipient of one of only 30 prestigious Acorn Awards, given to top restaurateurs under the age of 30 throughout the UK.

Trained as a chef at the Savoy Hotel in London, he set up in business in 1987 at the tender age of 25. Since then he has become something of a radio and television star, having presented 'Gourmet Food for Children' on BBC 1, appeared several times on Anglia TV, and has a weekly spot on radio Cambridgeshire/Peterborough. He is also a regular contributor to and subject of local, national and even international magazines and newspapers. Much attention has focused on his book, 'Serena's Choice' (after his daughter), which could be described as haute cuisine for children. It details many original, nutritious yet simple recipes for youngsters, all tested and approved by Serena herself.

However, Steven's mettle has been tested to the full by a tragedy which overtook The Pink Geranium in May 1991.....

SPECIAL NOTE ABOUT OUR FRONT COVER

Thatched roofs look marvellous, but are notoriously combustible. Sadly, that on The Pink Geranium proved no exception.

Undaunted, Steven has continued to serve to the same high standard at his private home, also a thatched cottage, just 50 yards away (tel. 0763 262503). Known as 'The Pink Geranium at Home', this arrangement should continue until Oct '91, when The Pink Geranium proper should be back in action.

Steven's brother, Stuart, is proprietor of the highly regarded 'Riverside Restaurant' in Woodbridge, Suffolk.

ASPARAGUS MOUSSE WITH SCALLOPS AND TARRAGON BEURRE BLANC (4 Covers)

With acknowledgements to **ADLARD'S, NORWICH**.

Ingredients:

2lb asparagus,
1/2 lb cleaned Scallops.

Ingredients for the mousse:

9ozs asparagus puree,
1/2 egg,
1 yolk,
2ozs double cream,
little lemon juice,
seasoning,
quatre epices (optional).

1. Cook the asparagus tips for garnish and refresh.
2. Cook the rest of the edible stalks to the puree stage. Refresh.
3. Puree them in the food processor and pass through a sieve. Add the rest of the ingredients.
4. Put them into twice buttered dariole moulds. Cover with foil.
5. Cook in a bain marie in a low oven 'til they are firm. (20 – 30 mins.)

Ingredients for the sauce:

2 big shallots finely diced,
7ozs dry white wine,
1tbsp double cream,
2ozs white wine vinegar,
8ozs unsalted butter,
Good bunch of chopped tarragon.

1. Reduce the shallots, wine and vinegar until dry.
2. Add cream, boil up and whisk in the butter gradually. Keep the sauce warm or it will separate.
3. Add tarragon and season.

To finish the dish:

1. Warm the asparagus tips and the muosse.
2. Put the sauce around the mousse.
3. In the meantime season the scallops and saute quickly in a non stick frying pan.
4. Arrange alternatively asparagus and scallops around the plate.
5. Serve.

SALMON TARTARE WITH A SMOKED SALMON MOUSSE
(serves eight)

With ackowledgements to **FRIARS RESTAURANT, SUDBURY**

Tartare

12 ozs salmon fillet
1 tbsp fresh dill
zest of 1/4 lemon, finely sliced
1 tbsp caster sugar
1/2 tsp Dijon mustard
2 tsp sour cream
lemon juice
salt & pepper

Prepare salmon 12 hours in advance.
Remove skin and tweeze out any bones. Place salmon on a large enough piece of clingfilm to enclose it. Mix together one tablespoon salt, the sugar, lemon zest and dill, and gently rub mixture into both sides of the salmon. Seal the clingfilm like a parcel and refrigerate for 12 hours. Unwrap salmon, rinse under cold water and pat dry. Cut into 1/8"cubes. In a bowl, mix together the mustard, sour cream, lemon juice and four turns of pepper, and mix in the salmon. Adjust seasoning.

Mousse

14 ozs smoked salmon trimmings
4 pinches cayenne pepper
juice of 1/2 lemon
1 pint whipping cream, chilled
salt
1/4 pint creme fraiche
1 tbsp chopped chives

Combine the smoked salmon, pinch of salt, cayenne and lemon juice in a food processor and puree for one minute only. With the processor on the lowest speed, slowly add half the chilled whipping cream. Force the puree through afine sieve and refrigerate for 10–15 mins. In a bowl, whip the remaining cream to a light peak and fold in the salmon puree. Refrigerate for two hours.

To arrange: make a circle of salmon tartare on each plate and quenelle two dessert of the salmon mousse in the centre. Decorate with a little creme fraiche sprinkled with a few chopped chives. Serve with melba toast.

VENISON, ONION & APRICOT COMPOTE

(for four persons)

With ackowledgements to **THE SWAN HOTEL, LAVENHAM**

ONION COMPOTE

1 large onion, finely chopped
1 tbsp white wine vinegar
1 tbsp honey
freshly milled black pepper
salt to taste
half glass of dry white wine

Put all ingredients into saucepan and cook until mixture is dry. Add salt and pepper to taste. Mixture should be quite piquant.

APRICOT FARCE

$^1/_4$ lb dried apricots
$^1/_2$ large onion
$^1/_2$ oz frsh white breadcrumbs
half glass dry white wine
$1^1/_2$ lbs eye saddle of venison

Roughly chop apricots, put into saucepan with the onions and wine. Cook gently until apricots are soft, bind with breadcrumbs and cool.

Cut saddle into four steaks. Using a steel make a hole through the centre of the eye of meat. Fill this with the farce.

SAUCE

2 juniper berries
1 shallot
1 sprig of fresh thyme
3 fl ozs orange juice
3 fl ozs red wine
1 oz redcurrant jelly
1 fl oz port
15 fl ozs game stock
1 oz unsalted butter

Place all the ingredients in a saucepan, except the butter. Reduce by half. Check consistency, finish with butter and pass through a fine strainer. Adjust seasoning.

CONVENT GARDEN TART

(for four persons)

With ackowledgements to **THE SWAN HOTEL, LAVENHAM**

12 ozs puff pastry
4 florets of cauliflower
4 florets of broccoli
2 ozs fine beans
2 ozs mange tout
8 pieces of baby corn
2 large carrots cut into battons
8 tips of asparagus
2 ozs button mushrooms, sliced and sauted

Roll out pastry and cut four circles seven inches in diameter. Bake for 15 mins. Remove from oven and cut off tops of each pastry and place back in the oven further three mins.

Cook all vegetables individually. Reheat and arrange on the pastry.

HERB HOLLANDAISE

3 egg yolks
8 ozs clarified butter
1 oz finely chopped herbs
basil
chives
sorrel
dill
parsley

Whisk egg yolks with few drops of water over a bain marie until white and thick. Remove from bain marie, slowly add tepid clarified butter whisking all the time. Add herbs and seasonings. Coat the vegetables with the sauce and glaze under the grill.

KING PRAWNS & SEASONAL VEGETABLES (for four)

Also from **THE SWAN HOTEL, LAVENHAM**

Ingredients

24 large king prawn tails
1 large carrot
2 small leeks
1 stick of celery
8 pieces of mange tout
1 courgette
sesame oil
soya sauce

Method

Remove shell from prawns, cut halfway through the prawn from the back to open them up like a butterfly. Remove dirt track and saute in a little sesame oil with salt and pepper. Arrange around outside of plate, sprinkle a little lemon juice over them.

Peel and wash vegetables and cut them into very fine strips about 3" long. Put a little sesame oil in a pan, saute the vegetables for about one minute, then add the soya sauce and seasonings. Place in centre of plate.

MEDALLIONS OF BEEF 'STOCKS'
(for four)

With ackowledgements to **PHIL VINCENT of STOCKS, BOTTISHAM**

Ingredients

2 ozs butter
4 x 6 ozs fillet steaks (cut into three slices)
4 ozs diced shallots
1 tsp chopped basil
3/4 pint espagnole (or brown beef sauce)
2 measures of whisky
1/4 pint double cream
4 ozs sliced mushrooms

Method

Lightly flatten the beef medallions. Fry in the butter lightly to seal. Remove from pan. Add shallots and sweat without colour. Add basil and brown sauce. Simmer, add mushrooms. Flame with whisky, finish sauce wth cream. Pour over medallions. Serve with boiled rice.

GRILLED SCALLOPS STUFFED WITH MUSSELS, WRAPPED IN BACON WITH A RHUBARB & GINGER SAUCE (serves four)

With ackowledgements to **THE DUKE OF YORK, BILLERICAY**

Ingredients

8 jumbo scallops
8 shelled mussels
4 rashers bacon
$^{1}/_{4}$ pint fish stock
1 oz butter
1 tbsp oil
1 lb rhubarb
$^{1}/_{4}$ pint fresh cream
white wine
fresh ginger
sugar to taste
seasoning

Method

Wash and drain scallops, dry in a cloth. Make an incision in centre of each scallop and stuff with a mussel. Cut rashers of bacon lengthways into eight strips. Wrap one strip around each scallop. Place on small baking tray with a little oil and butter, season and grill lightly on both sides until cooked. Put to one side.

For the sauce: wash and prepare rhubarb, poach in a little fish stock with sugar, white wine, some grated fresh ginger and a bayleaf. Cook until fruit is tender. Lightly liquidise to a puree consistency. Return to heat, add a little cream. Reduce, check seasoning and consistency. Finished sauce should be reddish pink. Napper sauce over arranged scallops, taking care not to completely cover them. Garnish and serve.

SEA TROUT & OYSTER IN MUSCADET JELLY WITH SHRIMP VINAIGRETTE (serves four)

With ackowledgements to **GARBO'S, KINGS LYNN**

Ingredients

8 oz fillet of sea trout
8 small or 4 large oysters, shucked, strained and reserved
1/2 bottle muscadet
1/2 sachet gelatine powder
1/2 star anise
salt

Vinaigrette

1/2 pint shrimps, peeled, heads and shells reserved
1 tbsp olive oil
1 small onion, finely chopped
1 carrot, finely chopped
1 stick celery, finely chopped
1 tbsp brandy
1 tbsp tomato puree
pinch Chinese 5–spice powder
zest 1/4 large orange
good olive oil
white wine vinegar

To make vinaigrette (may be stored in fridge. Serve at room temp.):–

Sweat shrimp and shells in tbsp olive oil in a heavy based pan for two mins. Add brandy and continue cooking until the smell of alcohol has gone. Remove heads and shells and reserve. Add finely chopped vegetables to the pan and cook until softened. Add back the shells and heads and tomato puree, 5–spice and orange zest, cover with cold water or fish stock and bring to the boil. Skim and simmer for 30–40 mins. Skim as necessary. Pass through a fine sieve, crushing the solids with the back of a spoon to extract all the liquid. Place the liquid into a clean pan and simmer until reduced by half. Remove from the heat and cool. When cool, measure and make a vinaigrette with the olive oil and vinegar in the following proportions:
1 part vinegar: 4 parts oil: 5 parts shrimp sauce.

Method

Gently poach the sea trout in half the quantity of wine with the star anise. Remove from the wine and leave to cool. Poach the oyster in the wine until just set. Remove from the liquid and allow to cool. Strain the wine through muslin and reboil. Remove from the heat and dissolve the gelatine powder in it. Pour this mixture into a measuring jug, add the remaining wine, oyster liquor (from shucking them) and salt to taste. You should have about a half pint. Leave to cool. Line four ramekins or other individual moulds with cling film. Flake the fish and divide it between the moulds, along with the oysters, tapping the moulds gently onto your work surface to avoid air bubbles. Place in fridge for about three hours until set.
To serve, turn out onto cold plates, surround with vinaigrette and garnish with reserved shrimps.

ROULADE OF DOVER SOLE WITH SMOKED SALMON & SORREL

(serves 2 main course or 4 starters)

With acknowledgements to **RECORDERS HOUSE RESTAURANT, THAXTED**

Ingredients

1 Dover sole 12 – 14 ozs, skinned & filleted
4 sorrel leaves
4 slices smoked salmon
4 ozs salmon mousse (see below)

Sauce

$^1/_4$ pint shrimp sauce
$^1/_4$ glass dry white wine
$^1/_4$ cup cream
2 sorrel leaves

Method

Line one square of tin foil with buttered greaseproof paper. Place two sole fillets face down on the paper. Spread the fillets with the salmon mousse. Top with sorrel leaves and then smoked salmon. Roll into a nice tight Swiss roll shape and seal both ends. Poach in lightly boiling water for approx. 10 – 12 minutes. Meanwhile, prepare the sauce.

Boil the shrimp sauce and white wine in a heavy pan. Allow to reduce slightly for approx. 5 mins. Remove from heat. Add the cream and finely shredded sorrel leaves. Reheat but do not boil. Carefully remove sorrel from the parcel. Place sauce on pre-heated dish. Slice sole thinly and arrange in a semi circle on the sauce. Garnish and serve.

SALMON MOUSSE

4 ozs fresh salmon
1 medium egg
$^1/_4$ glass dry white wine
$^1/_4$ tsp English mustard
salt & freshly ground black pepper
$^1/_4$ cup of cream

Place all ingredients except the cream in a food processor. Puree ingredients for a few minutes until smooth. Pass through a fine sieve. Gently add the cream. If mousse is slightly light set it on a bowl of ice for approx. 15 mins.

SALMON UNDER HORSERADISH CRUST IN RIESLING SABAYON

(serves four)

A simple but popular Austrian dish from **MANFRED HOLLWOGER, MIRABELLE, WEST RUNTON.**

Ingredients for crust

40g butter
1 dessertspoon lemon juice
cayenne pepper
2 dessertspoons grated horseradish
60g smoked salmon
100g fresh white breadcrumbs
4 slices wild salmon approx. 6 ozs each
salt
olive oil

Ingredients for sabayon

12cl (1/4 pint) fish stock
4cl riesling (dry, pref. from Alsace region)
2cl Noilly Prat
15cl double cream
cold butter
large spoon of whipped cream
cayenne & lemon juice to season

Method

Put salmon into cast iron casserole dish with drop of oil, colour quickly on each side. Prepare crust by creamin butter, add seasoning, diced smoked salmon, breadcrumbs. Make into paste, spread evenly over salmon. Put under grill until golden and finish in medium hot oven, but ensure it stays slightly underdone – insert cooking needle, leave for few seconds – should feel warm (not hot) to lips.

Sauce

Reduce fish stock over moderate heat, add riesling and Noilly Prat, reduce slightly and repeat with double cream. Add cold butter and whisk well, and finish with whipped cream to give creamy consistency. Put small ladle full on each hot plate. Sit salmon in centre, garnish with watercress and slice of smoked salmon. Serve immediately with leaf spinach and new potatoes.

FLASHED FRIED SCALLOPS WITH VEGETABLES AND THYME FLOWERS ON SAFFRON BUTTER SAUCE

With ackowledgements to **PULLMAN RESTAURANT, COLNE VALLEY RAILWAY, CASTLE HEDINGHAM.**

Ingredients for four

16 scallops (fresh in shells)
2 ozs each of finely sliced carrot, white leek, mange tout, red pepper
1 tbsp peanut oil
1 tsp dark sesame oil
1 tsp grated ginger
1 fresh bunch of thyme (with flowers if possible)
1 tbsp white wine vinegar
1 fl oz Noilly Prat
2 fl ozs white wine
½ pint double cream
pinch of saffron
2 ozs cold unsalted butter

Method

1. Remove scallops from shells – work over a bowl to retain juices.
2. Trim scallops – slice in half horizontally – reserve.
3. Prepare vegetables, cutting in to the finest strips possible.
4. Pass scallop juices through muslin to remove any grit. Place in a small saucepan with white wine, vinegar, Noilly Prat and thyme. Place on a high heat and reduce by four fifths. Add cream and simmer for one minute. Pass through a fine sieve and set aside in warm place.
5. Heat a large frying pan until VERY hot. Add oils, then 30 seconds later the scallops. Sear for 15 seconds, add vegetables and sautee vigorously for one minute. Tip into a colander to drain.
6. Whisk butter into the sauce a little at a time.
7. Place a mound of scallops and vegetables in the centre of the plate. Spoon the sauce around and decorate with thyme flowers. Serve.

KABANA POT (serves one)

With acknowledgements to **ANDREW WARD, CHEF at LE JARDIN RESTAURANT, GARDEN HOUSE HOTEL, CAMBRIDGE**

Ingredients

2 fresh smoked frankfurter sausages (do not use tinned variety)
1 oz button mushrooms
2 ozs grated gruyere cheese
1 fl oz white wine
1 oz butter
4 fl ozs double cream
pinch of freshly grated nutmeg
chopped parsley

Method

If possible, use a skillet frying pan, not only to prepare but also to serve.

1. Melt butter, toss sausages (chopped into 1" pieces) until warm.
2. Add quartered mushrooms, white wine and season with freshly ground black pepper.
3. Reduce until most of the liquid has evaporated.
4. Add the double cream and bring to the boil.
5. Stir in the cheese and simmer gently until rich and creamy.
6. Just before serving, grate a pinch of frsh nutmeg on top and sprinkle with chopped parsley.

Garlic bread is an excellent accompaniment.

BREAST OF GOOSE WITH CHESTNUT AND GRAND MARNIER SAUCE (serves four)

With acknowledgements to **JOHN HEALEY of SECKFORD HALL, NEAR WOODBRIDGE**

Ingredients

2 x 200g (1lb) raw goose breasts
100g whole chestnuts, cooked and peeled
150ml fresh double cream
75ml Grand Marnier

Marinade

80ml olive oil
10ml walnut oil
30ml white wine vinegar
2 cloves garlic
2 bay leaves
2 tblspns chopped celery
1 chopped carrot
1 tsp chopped tarragon
salt & pepper

Method

Mix together all of the marinade ingredients and allow to stand for 15 mins.

1. Score the skin of the goose breasts with a sharp knife to a depth of about 4mm.
2. Place in a deep dish and pour over the marinade. Cover and put in fridge for 72 hours.
3. Remove the goose breasts from the marinade and drain.
4. Seal goose breasts in hot saute pan. Cook in hot oven (gas mark 7) for approx. 5 mins until pink. Do not overcook.
5. Mix together the cream and Grand Marnier. Bring to the boil and cook quickly.
6. Slice goose breasts thinly and serve with the sauce.

VEAL ESCALOPE WITH STILTON & PRAWNS

(serves four)

With acknowledgements to **THE OLD MOOTE HOUSE, CASTLE HEDINGHAM**

Ingredients

4 x 5 ozs veal escalope
4 ozs stilton cheese
4 ozs prawns
white breadcrumbs
beaten egg
seasoned flour

Sauce

1 small bottle of tomato juice
1 lb peeled tomatoes
1 medium onion
$^1/_2$ tsp oregano
1 clove garlic
$^1/_2$ pint demi glace
$^1/_2$ glass med. dry red wine
clarified butter
parsley & lemon wedge to garnish

Method

To make the sauce, chop the tomatoes, finely dice onion, add to demi-glace, bring to bpoil, reduce to simmer for 10 mins, crush and finely chop the garlic, add to the sauce with the oregano, simmer for 5 mins, add wine to sauce just before serving.

Beat the escalopes out thinly, then place one ounce of stilton and one ounce of prawns on each, fold in half to form an envelope and seal round edges. Dip into seasoned flur, egg and breadcrumbs, shallow fry in the clarified butter until golden brown.

Nap sauce half over the veal, garnish with fresh parsley sprigs and wedges of lemon.

Accompany with new minted potatoes, mange tout, baby carrots, cauliflower florets.

SALMON MOUTARDE

With acknowledgements to **LITTLE HAMMOND'S, INGATESTONE**

Lightly poached quennnelles of fresh salmon, srved with a mustard and almond sauce, flamed with Amaretto.

Quennelles: 8oz of fresh boneless salmon,
1 egg white,
Salt and freshly ground black pepper,
Double cream for binding.

Sauce: 1oz flaked almonds,
Measure of Amaretto,
2 fl. ozs white wine,
$^1/_4$ pt. double cream,
1 finely chopped shallot,
Nob of butter,
Pinch of fresh chopped parsley,
Tablespoon course grain mustard

Stock: $^1/_2$ pt. white wine,
$^1/_2$ pt. water,
1 bayleaf, 6 whole peppercorns,
Dash of wine vinegar,
Nob of fish glace. (or small amount of fish stock).

Method:

Place the salmon into a food processor and blend for a few seconds, then add the egg whites and whip until light and fluffy. Add the seasoning and cream and blend. Shape into quennelles using two spoons. Put all the stock ingredients into a shallow pan and heat till simmering. Add quennelles and poach for two to three minutes until cooked.

Meanwhile, melt the butter in a pan, add shallots and almonds. When cooked, flame in Amaretto. Add wine, parsley, seasoning, mustard and finally cream. Cook until reduced by half. Pour sauce onto two plates, arrange quennelles on top and garnish.

The garnish used is a batter timbale filled with lightly poached leek and red pepper and mange tout, finished with caviar, chervil and rosemary with toasted almonds, and finally a shell on prawn.

Salmon Moutarde
at Little Hammonds, Ingatestone

LITTLE HAMMONDS NORTON CHICKEN

Supreme of chicken stuffed with a bacon and chicken mousseline inside a pastry lattice, roasted and served on a smoked bacon sauce.

Ingredients

For the farcis
1 x 6 ozs supreme of chicken (no wing bone)
2 slices of smoked bacon (no rind, bone or fat)
1 chopped shallot
1 egg yolk
Pinch of chopped parsley

For the pastry

2 – 3 ozs of puff pastry rolled out equally, flat approx 4mm.

For the sauce

2 slices of bacon in lardons (no rind, bone or fat)
1 fl oz white wine
$^1/_2$ pint single cream
$^1/_2$ tsp chicken glace
Salt and pepper

Method

Take the fillet off the chicken supreme and put it to one side for later. Take the supreme of chicken and push a sharp knife into the fat of the supreme, thus making a hole for the farcis to be piped into.

The farcis

Stage 1: robot chef the fillet of the supreme with the bacon, shallot, parsley, with one egg yolk and a touch of cream. Season with a pinch of both salt and pepper, and stuff into the supreme.

Stage 2: roll the pastry as above using a lattice cutter or by hand with a knife. Cut and stretch the pastry over the supreme and put on to the oven middle shelf to cook for 15 mins.

Stage 3: saute the shallots and smoked bacon without colour. Add the white wine, reduce by half and correct seasoning.

PAN FRIED BREAST OF MAIGRET DUCK WITH A HONEY & MANGO DRESSING (serves 4)

With acknowledgements to **KNAPTON HALL, NR NORTH WALSHAM, NORFOLK**

4 Maigret Duck breasts,
2 fresh mangoes
½ lb clear honey,
Lemon juice
Water,
Salt & pepper,
Apple, mint or watercress for decoration.

To make the dressing: peel 1 mango, remove the stone, place in a blender with the honey & lemon juice. Blend to a paste & dilute with water until runny. With second mango, peel and remove stone, but keep large enough to cut into slices.
Trim some of the excess fat from the duck breast, place into hot pan with a very small amount of fat to stop them sticking, cook until pink in the middle, about 7-8 mins, depending on size. When the duck is cooked remove from the pan and slice, inserting slices of mango between the duck, keep warm.
Place dressing into pan after draining the fat, heat the dressing until hot. Place duck in a fan on plate & pour the sauce into the centre of the fan. Decorate with fresh apple, mint or watercress.

MOHR IN HEMT WITH HOT CHOCOLATE SAUCE (serves 6- 8)

Another simple Austrian dish from **MANFRED HOLLWOGER, MIRABELLE, WEST RUNTON**

Ingredients:
100g plain chocolate
6 egg yolks
vanilla essence
100g caster sugar
100g ground hazelnuts
50g breadcrumbs
6 egg whites
little butter
icing sugar

Whip egg yolks with half of the caster sugar until frothy. Melt chocolate in sauce pan or microwave, add to egg mix. Mix hazelnuts and breadcrumbs together, set aside. Whip egg white with rest of caster sugar to stiff 'snow', and fold all together into egg yolk mix. Grease pudding bowl and dust in icing sugar, and fill to approx. ¾ of mould. Put into bain-marie and bake at 180¢c for 25 - 30 mins.
Meanwhile prepare hot chocolate sauce:

Ingredients for sauce:
4 fl ozs double cream
1 dessertspoon honey
vanilla essence
3 - 4 ozs plain chocolate

Bring double cream, vanilla essence and honey to boil, add chocolate (either in small pieces or pre-melted) with cream. Stir well, serve.
Dip chocolate pudding onto warm plate, pour chocolate sauce over, finish with dollop of whipped cream.

HOT SQUIDGY COFFEE & WALNUT SPONGE

With acknowledgements to **WEAVERS WINE BAR & EATING HOUSE, DISS**

Ingredients

12 ozs soft brown sugar
8 ozs butter
6 tbspns coffee essence
2 eggs
8 ozs self raising flour
1 pint milk
4 ozs walnut pieces

Method

Cream together 8 ozs of soft brown sugar with the butter until light and creamy. Beat together eggs & coffee essence, and add gradually to the creamed mixture. Add sieved flour & walnut pieces. Place in a deep buttered casserole dish.
Mix remaining sugar with milk and pour on top of sponge. Bake at 32°f for approx. 90 minutes.

ICED SAMBUCCA AND COFFEE SOUFFLE

With ackowledgements to **SALISBURY HOUSE, DISS**

Ingredients

½ pint whipping cream
6 ozs castor sugar
2 measures sambucca
6 egg whites
1 egg yolk
2 tsps instant coffee (mixed with a little hot water)

Method

1. Beat egg whites with 3 ozs sugar until firm.
2. Whip cream until soft peaks.
3. Mix all other ingredients to cream with wooden spoon.
4. Using a metal spoon, fold in egg whites to cream mixture.
5. Turn out into about eight individual souffle dishes or glases, and freeze for six hours.

Serve straight from the freezer, sprinkled with a little icicng sugar, and decorate with a few coffee beans or scrolls of chocolate.

SOUTHWOLD TART

Serves 6–8

With ackowledgements to **DAVID GOODE**, Chef de Cuisine, **THE SWAN HOTEL, SOUTHWOLD.**

Ingredients:

1 x 8" flan ring,
Sweet pastry, (see method)
8ozs plain flour,
4ozs sugar,
5ozs margarine,
1 egg (beaten)
6 x egg yolks,
1 x pt. double cream,
2 x tblsps of black treacle.

Method:

For sweet pastry:–

Mix the flour and the margarine until it forms breadcrumbs. Add the beaten egg and 2ozs of the sugar. Roll out to approximately 1/4" thick. Line an 8" flan ring and place the pastry in. Bake on Gas Mark 5–6 until lightly browned, before adding other ingredients.

For the filling:–

Whisk the six egg yolks and 2ozs of sugar.

Bring one pint of double cream to the boil. Add slowly to the egg mixture. Pour in a couple of tablespoons of black treacle and whisk well. Pass through a strainer.

Pour onto the sweet pastry in the flan ring and bake on a very low heat until the tart starts to set. Leave to cool, as it cools it will become firmer.

BAKED ROMAN CHEESECAKE

(serves 6 – 8)

With acknowledgements to **ANDY BUSH, THE GAMP RESTAURANT, FOULSHAM.**

Ingredients

1½ lb Philadelphia cheese
3 egg yolks well beaten
6 ozs caster sugar
2 ozs mixed peel
150ml dark rum
grated rind of lemon
pinch of salt

Method

Pre-heat oven to gas mark 8 or 230°c. Cream the Philadelphia cheese well into a large mixing bowl (on a machine if possible). Add egg yolks, sugar, peel lemon zest and salt, beat until mixture is smooth and then fold in rum. Turn into an 8" buttered and floured cake tin, bake in pre-heated oven for 15 mins, then at gas mark 5 or 200°c for a further 45 mins, or until the cheesecake is set and a wooden cocktail stick inserted into it comes out dry. Serve still warm, sprinkled with a little caster sugar with cinammon.

Andy Bush recommends that you serve it warm with rum and raisin icecream.

MRS WRIGHT'S BUTTERSCOTCH TART

With ackowledgements to **THE PUNCH BOWL, HIGH EASTER**

Ingredients

6 ozs dark brown sugar
6 ozs slated butter
½ pint condensed milk
14 ozs digestive biscuits & 4 ozs salted butter

Method

Line the base of a 7" flan case with the crushed biscuits by melting the butter, adding the biscuits and pressing firmly into the flan case, with a loose bottom to set.

To make the tart, melt the remaining 6 ozs of butter and the sugar VERY SLOWLY in a heavy based copper saucepan. When mixed together, add the milk and stir until all is combined. Slowly bring the mixture to the boil whilst being stirred, and when thickened pour onto flan case.

MIDSUMMER HOUSE

Midsummer Common, Cambridge. Tel. (0223) 69299

Hours: Open for lunch & dinner (last orders 9:30pm), Tues. – Fri. Dinner only Saturday. Sunday Lunch.

Credit cards: Access, Visa, Diners.

Price guide: 3 course set price £19.50. 6 course special £29.50. 2 course lunch £13.50. Sunday lunch £16.50.

Examples from menus (revised monthly): *carpaccio of scallop & wild salmon in dill vinaigrette, oyster mushroom with sweetbreads in tartlet shell; cucumber & yoghurt sorbet with mint; roulade of monkfish in pink butter sauce, supreme of guinea fowl in guava sauce with cocnut potatoes, rack of lamb with parsley crust & gratin potatoes.* Mousse *of dark & white chocolate, granite of apple in whisky sabayon with caramel ice.*

Decidedly cosmopolitan, Cambridge is yet quintessentially English – punts on the river, the lush meadows, huge commons bordered by the grand and dignified colleges – most evocative on a hot summer day. And it is on the edge of Midsummer Common, right on the banks of the Cam, that you will find this very English Victorian house, staffed mostly by young French people. His 'brigade', as Hans Schweizer (chef de cuisine and co-proprietor with TV presenter Chris Kelly) calls them, provide the friendly welcome. The cooking is universally recognised as quite outstanding, highly commended by national guides and journals. The garden (pictured) is a most agreeable spot for aperitifs on a long summer evening, and the dining room and conservatory are elegant without being at all 'stiff'. Fine upstairs room for private parties.

LE JARDIN RESTAURANT AT THE GARDEN HOUSE HOTEL

Granta Place, off Mill Lane, Cambridge. Tel. (0223) 63421

Hours:	Open for coffee, teas, light meals in the lounge, lunch & dinner (last orders 9:45pm).
Credit cards:	Access, Visa, Diners, Amex.
Price guide:	A la carte from £25, table d'hote lunch 11.95 (2 courses), £15.85 (3 courses). Sun lunch £16.35.
Accommodation:	118 rooms, all en suite, with full facilities. AA & RAC **** From £77 single, £108 double.

Examples from menus: *truffle scented game consomme baked with a puff pastry lid, skillet of jumbo mussels with pernod & cream; succulent meats carved from trolley, Szechuan lamb stir fried with oyster sauce (served with chopsticks), pastry horn of shellfish with saffron & seaweed sauce, wild venison cutlet with lemon grass sauce. Crepes suzettes flambeed at table.*

Situated in beautiful riverside gardens with views over open meadows, this luxury four star hotel is yet just two minutes' walk from the city centre. Guests are pampered in style, from the moment they enter the cool marbled entrance hall to retiring to the superbly appointed bedrooms (many with balconies overlooking the river and meadows beyond). Far superior to normal hotel fare, Le Jardin offers truly international cuisine with imaginative dishes and an excellent wine list. Chef Andrew Ward creates a new and exciting recommendation menu for both lunch and dinner every week. An unbeatable breakfast buffet is available to non-residents as well, and the hotel has exceptionally good conference and business facilities.

SLEPE HALL HOTEL

Ramsey Road, St. Ives Tel. (0480) 63122

Hours: 12 to 2pm, 7 to 9:30pm (9pm Sundays), 7 days, restaurant and bar meals.

Credit cards: Access, Visa, Diners, Amex.

Price guide: A la carte £19.50 Table d'hote from £9.50 Sun. lunch £9.95.

Accommodation: 16 rooms (15 en suite).

Examples from menus (a la carte revised 4–6 months, table d'hote weekly): *courgette & brie soup, smoked ham & chestnut terrine; salmon & sole roulade with chive butter sauce, breast of maigret duck in green peppercorn sauce, fillet of beef Rossini, noisette of lamb (in beansprout, mushroom & oyster sauce), aubergine pizzaiola. Bar meals: steak & venison pie, steak & kidney pudding, smoked haddock & asparagus crumble, sweet & sour pork, chicken curry. Homemade desserts.*

"There is no love sincerer than the love of good food" – George Bernard Shaw's pithy observation is quoted on the menu. A small country hotel cannot afford to rely on residents alone to fill the restaurant, so food is taken seriously. Like many of the best establishments, this one is family owned, and under the personal supervision of resident manager Bob Hardy. Chef Andrew Searle was the country's youngest to gain his City & Guilds. The opulent dining room is far above normal hotel standards, in an elegant building that was once a girls' school. St. Ives, formerly known as 'Slepe', is an attractive lively riverside town, close to Cambridge, Ely and the A1, and so well placed for business or pleasure. The ballroom can accommodate functions up to 200, and The Cromwell Room up to 40.

THE POSTE GROUP

Hours:	Open for coffee, lunch & dinner (tea also at Haycock & Old Bridge), last orders 10pm. Bar meals lunch & evening.
Credit cards::	Access, Visa, Diners, Amex.
Price guide:	A la carte from about £20. Bar meals from around £2.50.
Accommodation:	53 en suite rooms at Haycock, 26 en suite at Old Bridge.

The Three Horseshoes, Madingley
Tel: (0954) 210221

Examples from menus: **Three Horseshoes** – *pickled cod with avocado, light crab cakes with scallops in sauce scented with ginger.* **Old Bridge** – *terrine of Aylesbury duck & fresh sage with ginger marmalade, fillet of pork with caramelised onions & baked apple.* **Haycock** – *stir fry of mange tout & prawns, sauted breast of chicken with leaf spinach & rosemary sauce.* **Pheasant** – *quail egg & smoked salmon ravioli, magret of duck with tangy apricot & brandy sauce.*

One of the most prestigious groups in the region, and well known beyond, especially **The George at Stamford, tel. (0780) 55171** (not featured here as it's in Lincolnshire). The Haycock is a beautiful mellow stone 17th century coaching inn on the old A1, in a very pretty village. The Three Horseshoes, just outside Cambridge, is an uncommon combination of lively pub and sophisticated restaurant, noted for seafood. The Pheasant is the idyllic village green thatched pub, but also boasts a class restaurant. The Old Bridge, a splendid Georgian house and a local landmark, is superbly well appointed throughout. All feature regularly in the major guides.

Pheasant, Keyston Tel: (080 14) 241

Haycock, Wansford
Tel: (0780) 782223

Old Bridge Hotel, Huntingdon
Tel: (0480) 52681

OPHELIA'S

10 The Causeway, Godmanchester. Tel. (0480) 450413

Hours: 11:30am to 2:15pm Mon – Fri, 7 pm until late Mon – Sat.
Credit cards: Access, Visa, Mastercard, Diners, Amex.
Price guide: A la carte lunch & dinner £20. Table d'hote dinner £18.50 (4 courses), £23 (6 courses); lunch £7.95 (2 courses), £10.95 (3 courses).

Examples from menus (a la carte revised seasonally, table d'hote lunch weekly, dinner fortnightly): *prawn & avocado timbale set on lobster mayonnaise, chicken & vegetable terrine on orange & tomato coulis; peach & passion fruit sorbet; grilled red mullet on bed of pan fried snow peas in lemon butter, venison 'Ophelia' (collops in port wine & elderflower vinegar sauce), pancake trio on honey & almond sauce (filled with asparagus & lime, mixed beans, fruit compote), steak au poivre. Strawberry filled choux swans on raspberry lake, meringue 'Ophelia' (nest filled with hot fruits of the forest laced with brandy & fresh cream), bread & butter pudding.*

To open a restaurant and make it a success in such austere times requires not only nerve but also high standards. Co-proprietors Richard Brook and Danny Mountain (chef) have each 15 years experience to call on, working at The Ritz, Hilton and other top establishments. They found this little timber beamed black and white Elizabethan (1597) gem (overlooking the Little River Ouse) somewhat dilapidated, but have refurbished to achieve a rare combination of elegant refinement in an informal, friendly atmosphere. Cuisine could be described as classic French in modern English style, always with vegetarian alternatives. French country wines are a speciality. Private parties (up to 26) welcome.

THE GEORGE HOTEL

High Street, Ramsey, nr Huntingdon. Tel. (0487) 815264

Hours: 12 to 2pm, 7 to 9:30 pm daily.
Credit cards: Access, Visa, Diners, Amex.
Price guide: A la carte £15, table d'hote £11.95, lunch £5.50.
Accommodation: 11 rooms en suite. Tv's, telephones.

Examples from menu: *queen scallops in white wine sauce, chef's chicken liver pate on Cumberland sauce; lemon sole Duglare (fillets poached in cream & pepper sauce, garnished with prawns), chicken fromage (supreme cooked in port & cheese sauce), veal a la creme, beef stroganoff, steaks, seasonal vegetables in garlic cream sauce in puff pastry case, nut loaf.*

Perhaps the only town centre hotel to overlook a golf course (to the rear), the George has been a focal point in this pleasant little Fenland town since about 1600. Now under the ownership of the Miles family (who also own the well known Bell Hotel in Clare), it was recently restored and refurbished to a high standard. Before dining, sip an aperitif in the long, well appointed lounge or cocktail bar. Then into Knights Restaurant, which combines spaciousness with intimacy. Here one is presented with a very reasonably priced yet varied menu, prepared by chef Clive Stewart, accompanied by a balanced wine list. Bedrooms are comfortable and well equipped, a function room accommodates up to 80, there's access to the golf club and a leisure centre, plus ofcourse all the traditional country pursuits, so one is well placed here (not far from Cambridge or Peterborough) for business or pleasure. Parking for 40.

THE LAMB HOTEL & OCTAGON RESTAURANT

2 Lynn road, Ely. Tel. (0353) 663574

Hours: 12 to 2pm, 7 to 10pm, 7 days. Lounge open all day for snacks.

Credit cards: Access, Visa, Diners, Amex.

Price guide: A la carte £16, table d'hote £13.50. Sunday lunch £9, 'Tourist's lunch' £6.00.

Accommodation: 13 twins, 5 doubles, 5 American twins, 2 four posters, all with full facilities. From £55 single,£72 double. Weekend breaks £35 pp per night.

Examples from menus (revised periodically): *mild creamed curried prawns, pasta & aubergine stir fry; lemon sole nabuchu (with avocado, asparagus & mushroom sauce), crisp sliced breast of duckling in honey & lemon sauce, baked lamb fillets sevillane (coated in marinated apricots, baked in puff pastry, served with tangy apricot sauce, steaks, kidney bean casserole. Daily sweets.*

Healthy eating is much more than a mere passing fad, and can be of enough concern to deter many people from eating out. The management of The Lamb (a member of Queens Moat Houses) takes the subject very seriously, and the healthy eating theme is clearly evident on the menu – dishes are coded with 'V' for vegetarian and with a heart for 'healthy'. Obviously the restaurant is more than just an adjunct to the hotel, and must stand on its own merit. In warm pink and elegantly furnished, it commands a good view of Ely Cathedral, just yards away, and one of England's finest. The beautiful Oak Room is now reserved for meetings, and a new bright cocktail lounge has taken its place. As a 15th century coaching inn, The Lamb has long been the hub of business and social life of this village-sized city. The buttery is open all day for snacks, or just drop by for morning coffee or afternoon tea. The bedrooms are very well appointed, and there are full facilities for conferences, receptions etc.

THE FENHOUSE RESTAURANT

2 Lynn Road, Littleport, nr Ely. Tel. (0353) 860645

Hours: 7 to 9pm (last orders). Sunday lunch.
Credit cards: Access, Visa, Diners.
Price guide: A la carte £23 average. Sun. lunch £13.50.

Examples from menus (revised monthly): *julienne of pigeon breast served on bed of brown lentils, light salad of crab & asparagus with chive vinaigrette, quails eggs served on nest of leek & smoked salmon with smoked cod's roe sauce; breast of duck with calvados & nutmeg sauce & apple tartlet, coulibiac of mushrooms & rice & spinach with herb butter sauce. Blood orange sorbet with praline chocolate mousse, fine shortbread biscuits layered with lemon syllabub & strawberries with raspberry coulis.*

Michelin and other major guides continue to laud this little 22 seater gem, which will be heartily endorsed by its many admirers, including a number of fellow restaurateurs. David and Gaynor Warne have worked hard over four years to earn this recognition for their 17th century cottage out in the 'wilds' of Fenland. One may arrive by car, boat or train (the river and station are very near), but can always look forward to a well considered and balanced menu prepared by David himself, and a friendly reception from Gaynor, who brought with them nearly 20 years of experience. All is fresh and homemade, even bread and ice cream, and many of the vegetables are organically grown. 50 or so wines appear on a very good list.

THE RED HOUSE RESTAURANT

45 Mill Street, Isleham, nr Ely. Tel. (0638) 780453

Hours: 7 to 9:30pm (flexible), Tues – Sat. Sun lunch 12 to 2pm. Other lunches by appointment.

Credit cards: Access, Visa, Switch.

Price guide: A la carte £15. Sun lunch £10.

Examples from menus (revised seasonally): *mini cheese fondue, crispy duck & asparagus salad, terrine of fresh salmon & langoustine served warm with cucumber & dill sauce; light fish curry, fillets of brill topped with crabmeat & fresh herb crust served with chervil and Muscadet cream sauce, roast guinea fowl with hazelnut stuffing, peppered sirloin steak with brandy & cream sauce, fillet of lamb & wild mushrooms served with tarragon & mint flavoured madeira sauce, medallions of pork (in calvados, chive & orange cream sauce), mushroom stroganoff. Homemade desserts.*

A welcome addition to the Cambridgeshire scene, this striking red listed building (1848) houses not only an elegant restaurant, but also offers professional conference facilities and private dining room, and makes a lovely setting for a wedding reception – many a newlywed has posed for a photograph at the top of the magnificent staircase. In summer one can sip aperitifs on the patio or lawns, overlooked by restaurant and terrace, and perhaps identify some of the 25 herbs grown in the garden. Vegetarian dishes are a speciality, and ofcourse only the very freshest produce is used. Isleham is a peaceful little village, yet is only minutes from the A45 and Newmarket, Mecca of racing. Good parking. Coach parties welcome for afternoon tea. Outside catering service.

STOCKS RESTAURANT

76 High Street, Bottisham, Cambridge Tel. & Fax (0223) 811202

Hours: Lunch from 12pm except Mondays & Saturdays.
Dinner from 7pm except Sundays & Mondays

Credit cards: Access, Visa.

Price guide: A la carte from £16.50, table d'hote (Tues–Fri) £16.50. Lunch from £6. Sunday lunch £9.20 (3 courses).

Examples from menus (revised seasonally): *cornets of smoked salmon filled with prawn mousse, avocado fruits de mer, mushrooms in port & stilton sauce; supreme de canard cerise, medallions of beef 'Stocks', salmon en croute with hollandaise, scampi a la croix. Strawberry mille feuille. Sundays: always a rib of beef, bread & butter pudding, treacle pud.*

Dickie Jeeps C.B.E., co-proprietor with wife Jenny, is a former captain of the England rugby side, hence the badges and international shirts on display. Built in 1478, this is the oldest house in the village, far more attractive inside than out. Open fires warm the two beamed reception lounges and beautifully appointed dining room, now completely redecorated and furnished. 'The Winter Garden' is a large, bright conservatory (overlooking swimming pool), with its own disco, and in demand for private functions. The food is also very good! The American newspaper, Stars and Stripes, awarded its highest ever rating of an English restaurant. Chef Philip Vincent, who has appeared on tv, is skilled in the art of lard and margarine carvings, and also produces super cakes for weddings and other special occasions (seating up to 80, buffet 100). Large, interesting wine list includes some unusual South Africans. Located opposite church in Bottisham, just off A1303.

QUY MILL RESTAURANT & HOTEL

Stow-cum-Quy, Newmarket Road, nr Cambridge. Tel. (0223) 853383
Fax (0223) 853770

Hours: 12 to 2:00pm, 7:30 to 9pm (not Sun evening). Bar meals lunch & evening, 7 days. Morning coffees, afternoon teas.
Credit cards: Access, Visa, Diners.
Price guide: A la carte £20 – £25, table d'hote £16 – £18. Bar £3 – £6.
Accommodation: 2 singles (£58.50), 24 double/twins (£75), all with full facilities (1 for disabled), 2 with 4-posters. Tourist Board 4 crowns.

Examples from menus (revised 2 or 3 times weekly): *oeufs poche au jambon, casolet escargots au champignons; fruits de mer en croute, Quy Mill fillet steak in brandy cream sauce with julienne of peppers, grilled red snapper, rigatoni Napolitana. Homemade sweets. Bar: steak & kidney yorkies, lasagne, chilli, aubergine bake, fish pie, fresh trout.*

Chef Jonathan Swann has cooked for royalty (including the king of Sweden), and his versatility is evident from an everchanging menu, highlighted by monthly special evenings, such as Caribbean, for example. The Domesday Book mentions a mill on this site, but this one dates 'only' from the 17th century. The waterwheel, lit up at night, is quite a spectacle in the restaurant, though sadly it is not turning at the moment after the spate of dry summers. Though only a few hundred yards from the busy A45, the hotel stands sheltered and peaceful in 14 acres of grounds, including a very pleasant lawned garden. It is a marvellous venue for a wedding reception, but having three conference rooms is also perfect for a business function. Cambridge, Ely and Newmarket are very near, and animals are welcome in the hotel's own kennels.

MAGUIRE'S RESTAURANT & WINE BAR (& SWAN HOUSE INN)

High Street, Fowlmere. Tel. (0763) 208444

Hours: 12 to 2:30pm, 7 to 10pm (not Sun. evenings). Bar meals lunch & evening 7 days, wine bar also.
Credit cards: Access, Visa, Amex.
Price guide: A la carte set price £15.50 & £19. Sunday lunch £9.75.

Examples from menus (revised monthly): *woodland pigeon chef's style (breasts beaten out, well seasoned, spread with duck farce, rolled, poached, served with piquant sauce), fan of avocado with baby artichokes & palm hearts served with mint vinaigrette; vol au vent filled with mixture of monkfish & prawns (flamed with cognac, in rich creamy sauce), Pickwick pie (beef fillet, gammon, mushrooms, oysters in special sauce), vegetable strudel. Homemade desserts or cheeseboard.*

Whatever the mood or occasion, one of this uncommon trio is bound to satisfy. The Swan freehouse is the one for a good pint and wholesome bar food, in a cheering atmosphere. The bright and lively wine bar offers an excellent wine list (with descriptions by the proprietor), and more sophisticated light meals – ideal for lunch, perhaps. The quality restaurant is for those seeking a gastronomic experience in elegant surrounds. The cuisine is Anglo-French, painstakingly prepared from fresh ingredients, and beautifully presented. Three different functions under the one ancient roof, and just a short drive south of Cambridge. Children accepted in wine bar and restaurant. Outside catering a speciality.

THE PINK GERANIUM

Station Road, Melbourn. Tel. (0763) 260215

Hours: Open for lunch & dinner, Tues. – Sat., plus Sunday lunch.
Credit cards: Access, Visa.
Price guide: A la carte £25. Table d'hote lunch £14.95.

Examples from menus (revised seasonally): *souffle of wild mushrooms with saffron sauce, pan-fried foie gras on toasted brioche with caramelised baby onions & citrus jus; trio of fish (teryaki of tuna, home smoked salmon, king prawn provencale with garden herbs), Pink Geranium crispy duck, fillet of English lamb with celeriac timbale, rosti of venison, blanquette of turbot with baby vegetables, ample vegetarian options.*

It seems the Pink Geranium goes from strength to strength – frequented by celebrities, film stars and even royalty. Proprietor Steven Saunders has himself become a 'celebrity chef', appearing often on both BBC radio and television food shows. Great emphasis is placed on high quality food and presentation, everything being home made. In summer, herbs and vegetables come straight from the garden. Since the last edition, yet more praise has been heaped (see page 4), in part due to his flair for inventive ideas, such as the Rolls Royce and Jaguar Service, to collect and return clients home (book in advance), plus a creche, enabling parents to enjoy a superb lunch or dinner in peace! Steven is always there to greet guests personally, indicative of the warm and friendly atmosphere of this unique establishment.
NEWS FLASH A devastating fire in May '91 has caused a temporary move just 50 yards to Steven and Sally's home, a similar 16th century thatched cottage in one acre of gardens (tel. 0763 262503). The original re-opens November '91.

SHEEN MILL HOTEL & RESTAURANT

Station Road, Melbourn. Tel.(0763) 261393
Fax (0763) 261376

Hours: 12:30 to 2pm, 7:30 to 10pm. Morning coffees. Bar meals lunchtimes only.
Credit cards: Access, Visa, Diners, Amex.
Price guide: A la carte £22 – £25. Lunch £13.50.
Accommodation: 4 doubles, 4 singles, all en suite.

Examples from menus (revised seasonally): *grilled brochette of angel fish wrapped in smoked bacon with herb & garlic butter, asparagus mousseline with leek & tomato sauce garnished with asparagus & chervil; fillets of Dover sole wrapped around smoked salmon served on light chablis & lobster sauce, fillet steak filled with veal mousse served with brandy & oyster mushroom sauce, breast of duck with apricot & sage stuffing on pomegranate & apple sauce, flambes, vegetarian dishes, cuisine minceur (for slimmers).*

The photograph can barely do justice to one of the prettiest riverside settings in the region. The bedrooms of this 17th century mill all overlook this delightful canvas, and all guests can enjoy it from the pleasant conservatory, perched on the water's edge. In the elegant peach, cream and grey restaurant (also with fine views), superb food is presented under the direction of Tim Wainright-Noble, whose career has been linked with such celebrated names as Simpson's on The Strand, The Royal Garden and The Empress, and more recently as executive chef at the five star Carlton Hotel, and Maxim's de Paris. Tim's menus are based on modern classical French cuisine, using only the finest fresh produce, which has secured a place in Michelin and other major good food guides. Low calorie and vegetarian dishes are featured in keeping with modern trends, but all special requirements are met with care and personal attention.

GREEN END PARK HOTEL

Dane End, nr Ware. Tel. (0920) 438344/438780

Hours: 12 to 3pm, 7 to 9:30pm daily.
Credit cards: Access, Visa, Diners, Amex.
Price guide: A la carte £25, table d'hote £22.50, lunch £17.50.
Accommodation: 10 bedrooms, all with full facilities. Special weekend packages.

Examples from menus (revised 6 monthly): *warm scallops with truffle served with light champagne sauce, marbre of trout leek & salmon with pepper coulis, pan fried chicken liver & bacon with young leaf salad & vegetable tagliatelle; chicken ballotine with almonds & creamed mustard sauce, entrecote steak flavoured by girole sauce, vegetable chartreuse filled with chestnut mousse. Trad. Sun. roasts. Light lunches in restaurant or on terrace.*

Standing in eight acres of beautiful landscaped gardens, this elegant 18th century manor house is eminently suitable as a base for touring or business, being only minutes from the M25, M11, A1 and A10. The rooms are of a grace and proportion sadly lacking in most modern hotels – the splendid restaurant, overlooking the gardens and topiary, retains many original features, including ornate cornice work by Italian craftsmen. Three stylish meeting rooms come well equipped for business functions, and in summer wedding receptions make a fine spectacle in the garden, terrace or marquee. Lawn tennis, croquet and an 18 hole putting green (equipment provided) are amusing and relaxing diversions. But even if you're not staying, the restaurant (with well stocked cellar) is well worth a visit.

REDCOATS FARMHOUSE HOTEL

Redcoats Green, nr Hitchin. Tel. (0438) 729500
Fax (0438) 723322

Hours: 12 to 1:30pm, 7 to 9pm, except Sat. lunch, and for special occasions only on Sundays. Bar meals lunchtimes except weekends.
Credit cards: Access, Visa, Diners, Amex.
Price guide: A la carte £24. Bar snacks/meals from £5.
Accommodation: 14 en suite rooms with TV. & phone. From £55 single, £65 double. Special weekend rates.

Examples from menus (revised every Tuesday): *smoked eel with horseradish sauce, parma ham with fresh figs, mushrooms 'Armenienne' (with garlic, bacon, walnuts & pepper); fresh hake cutlet (with prawns, white wine, parsley & cream), half Gressingham duckling with apple & drambuie sauce, game from own or other local estates, fillet steak topped with asparagus & gruyere cheese, savoury nut cutlets in filo pastry with fresh tomato sauce. Homemade puddings.*

You'd never guess, here in the rolling Hertfordshire countryside, that you were only 35 miles from London, and just minutes from the A1. The farmhouse has stood peacefully since the 1400's, and has been in the Butterfield family for generations, but was made an hotel only in 1970 by Peter and sister Jackie. Old English charm exudes: antiques and paintings, open fireplaces, exposed beams. The individual bedrooms are in the house or in a converted stable block. Some of them look out over pretty gardens, where marquees are erected for weddings – business functions are also well catered for. In the three dining rooms one can expect traditional English and continental cuisine, augmented by fresh local produce. Nearly 200 wines make up the cellar. Rated by main guides. Outside catering a speciality.

THE HARPENDEN MOAT HOUSE HOTEL

18 Southdown Road, Harpenden. Tel. (0582) 764111

Hours: 12 to 2pm, 7 to 10pm daily.
Credit cards: Access, Visa, Diners, Amex, Eurocard, Air Plus.
Accommodation: 53 bedrooms, all en suite, incl. 2 executive rooms, 3 bridal suites, 2 apartments.

Examples from menus (revised four monthly): *warm salad of wood pigeon & wild mushrooms on bed of seasonal leaves, terrine of salmon sole & lobster on light watercress sauce; tournedos of beef enhanced with smoked oysters on two wine sauces, sliced breast of duck with goooseberry tartlet on marsala jus, salmon marinated in ginger poached & served with slices of mango. White chocolate terrine with vanilla sauce, praline parfait on bed of toffee sauce.*

Harpenden is one of Hertfordshire's most agreeable towns (close to M1, M25, A1). Overlooking the Common, this prestigious hotel prides itself in offering the best of Hertfordshire hospitality. Formerly St Dominic's Convent, the 300-year-old manor house has been tastefully converted to afford facilities and standards of comfort to satisfy the most discerning traveller. After sipping aperitifs in the stylish Cocktail Bar or Piano Lounge, take your seat in the elegant 'Georgian Restaurant', sumptuously appointed, as can be seen in the photograph. Here one is presented with cuisine of the highest order, the accent very much on fresh produce in the creation of imaginative dishes. Good food is best enjoyed in an informal atmosphere, and is enhanced by the gracious surroundings. Ideal whether on business or pleasure.

ST. MICHAEL'S MANOR HOTEL & RESTAURANT

Fishpool Street, St. Albans. Tel. (0727) 864444

Hours: 12:30 to 2pm, 7 to 8:30pm, 7 days.
Credit cards: Access, Visa, Diners, Amex.
Price guide: A la carte £22, table d'hote from £18, lunch £16.
Accommodation: 22 bedrooms, all en suite.

Examples from menus (revised daily): *smoked salmon & halibut platter, spinach tagliatelle (with tomato, peppers & wild mushrooms; fillet of plaice breaded & lightly grilled with banana, Washington guinea fowl (with Chinese sweetcorns & asparagus tips), Canadian lobster, tournedos St Michaels, noisettes of lamb on redcurrant coulis. sweets from trolley.*

In the heart of the old Roman town of Verulamium (once England's capital), this superb Tudor (1586) manor stands in five acres of quite magnificent gardens with large lake, overlooked by a terrace and Victorian conservatory (which forms part of the restaurant). Though a very characterful, distinguished house, the atmosphere is never less than friendly and attentive, the mark of a family hotel – proprietors Michael and Gladys Newling Ward have just celebrated 26 years here, Martin Richardson is resident director and Andrew Billington is the manager. Chef Steven Juett maintains a first rate reputation for the restaurant, popular with business people and families. Outstanding venue for functions, weddings etc.

THE SALISBURY RESTAURANT

15 The Broadway, Old Hatfield. Tel. (0707) 262220

Hours: Dinner Tues – Sat, lunch Tues – Fri, plus Sunday.
Credit cards: Access, Visa, Diners, Amex.
Price guide: A la carte £25, table d'hote £18, lunch £15.

Examples from menus (revised seasonally, table d'hote daily): *wild mushroom & watercress soup with fresh cream, chicken liver parfait set on redcurrant & red wine sauce served with melba toast; fresh water perch filled with Cornish crab meat (wrapped in spinach leaves & set on watercress sauce), best end of lamb set on orange & madeira sauce scented with fresh garden herbs. White chocolate souffle with Grand Marnier, trio of fruit sorbets in brandy snap biscuit set on strawberry & port wine sauce.*

Old Hatfield is a pleasant little town, blessed with a restaurant of the first order. A former coaching inn, it has for 150 years provided for the needs of travellers on the Great North Road on which it stands. Standards of comfort in the lounge bar and stylish air conditioned dining room far surpass those known to travellers past, as indeed does the modern English cuisine. Fiona Gulliver became owner in December '88, and with manager Michael Regan and chef Kevin Wright continue to establish an enviable reputation, recognised by major national guides – a much needed highlight of the Hertfordshire scene. Exceptionally good wine list. Private car park.

THE GABLE HOUSE RESTAURANT

Newgate Street Village, Cuffley. Tel. (0707) 873899

Hours:	7.30 to 9.30pm Mon – Fri, 7.30 to 10.30pm Sat. 12.30 to 2pm Mon – Sat, 12.30 to 4pm Sun.
Credit cards:	Access, Visa, Diners, Amex.
Price guide:	A la carte £25, table d'hote £14.50. Lunch £10.50 & £12.50 for 2 and 3 courses.
Accommodation:	2 doubles £45 per room incl.

Examples from menus (a la carte revised 8 weekly, lunch & table d'hote daily): *stuffed calamari with fresh herb & tomato sauce, fresh asparagus in puff pastry garnished with asparagus tips and wine butter; supreme of chicken filled with apple & walnut mousse on madeira sauce, duet of salmon & sea bream in fish cream sauce, sirloin steak with black pudding & onion rings. Quenelles of strawberry fool on spiders web of chocolate, sponge & date pudding with caramel sauce.*

Although on the borders of London this is a green and peaceful area, and it would be hard to find better accommodation at such reasonable rates. Hatfield House is quite close, and there's good riding to be had, whether on horseback or Shank's pony. Built in 1907, the house is of a striking and unusual design, and inside is airily decorated in pinks and apricots. Cuisine may be described as modern English, utilising the best of fresh produce form the London markets – everything, including icecreams, is home made. For extra interest, look out for the periodic special evenings, such as Austrian or French Loire. As well as an excellent wine list, proprietors Messrs Deering and Judge proffer a complete range of vintage ports from 1934 to 1985. Rated by many major guides.

THE CRICKETERS ARMS

Rickling Green & Quendon, nr Saffron Walden. Tel. (0799 88) 595
Fax (0799 88) 512

Hours:	12 to 2pm, 7 to 9:30pm, 7 days. Sun. lunch 12:30 to 3pm.
Credit cards:	Access, Visa, Amex.
Price guide:	Set price menus 15.50 & 17.50.
Accommodation:	7 rooms, all with full facilities. From £50 per room, incl.

Examples from menus (revised seasonally): *moules mariniere, crudites, poached egg on bed of smoked haddock (topped with a cream & smoked salmon sauce); salmon 'Josephine' (supreme cooked in raisin & ginger butter, wrapped in puff pastry, baked and served with herb cream), 'duck in the mud' (breast grilled, served with rich sauce of dried fruits, brandy, lemon juice & cream), vegetarian pancakes. Homemade sweets.*

Essex county cricket side plays here one Friday every June, and if you want to know more, proprietors Tim and Jo Proctor will gladly send a quarterly fixtures list. On this you will also find three different set price menus (about five choices for each course), prepared from only the very freshest ingredients (bought by Tim at the London markets) by Jo and young chef David, trained 'in house'. The restaurant (which now shares an entrance with the hotel) was extended recently to 70 covers (special occasion bookings welcome). Thursday is 'trial night', a chance to test his creations at just £9.95 for three courses. Do not be put off by a slightly forbidding Victorian frontage; behind it is a quite charming beamed Tudor interior. The accommodation is of a very high standard, and one can expect a restful night in this peaceful situation, only minutes from the M11 and Stansted Airport.

THE OLD HOOPS

15 King Street, Saffron Walden. Tel. (0799) 22813

Hours: 12 to 2:15pm, 7 to 10pm, Tues. – Sat.
Credit cards: Access, Visa, Diners, Amex.
Price guide: A la carte £15 – £20. Lunch £7 – £12.

Examples from menus (revised quarterly, plus daily specials): *melon filled with raisins & apricots in a sweet brandy sauce, avocado pear with marinated mushrooms, smoked breast of turkey with pine kernel & almond vinaigrette; lamb Dijonnaise (fillet wrapped in spinach & bacon, lightly roasted, sliced and served with mild Dijon mustard sauce), breast of chicken stuffed with smoked salmon in champagne sauce, poached fillet of codling with parsley sauce. Chocolate parfait, strawberry diamonds (fresh baked puff pastries filled with cream flavoured with orange liqueur, topped with fanned strawberries, served with chilled custard sauce), mango & lime mousse.*

Saffron is the world's most expensive spice, and this pleasant little town was once the centre of trade. Also highly valued but far from expensive, 'The Hoops' can be found right in the middle of the main street, and being on the first floor one can reflect on passing street life whilst digesting the best of fresh food prepared to order. Dating from the 14th century and once a pub, informality still prevails – chef patron Ray Morrison prefers it that way, even though he worked in top West End clubs. With his own style of cooking and attention to detail, he and his family have built an excellent reputation over a number of years, earning a regular spot in national guides. There's no minimum spend, and the wine list is modestly priced – unlike some of the menus in a fascinating collection from all over the world, pinned around the walls. Booking advisable at weekends.

LANTERN COTTAGE

Howlett End, Wimbish. Tel. (0371) 830865

Hours: 12 to 2pm Tues – Fri & Sun, 7 to 9pm Tues – Sat.
Credit cards: Access, Visa
Price guide: 2 course dinner £16, 3 course £18, 4 course £20. Lunch from £12. Sun lunch £8 (2 courses), £9.50 (3 courses).

Examples from menus (revised seasonally): *half barbary duck roasted & served with orange & lemon sauce laced with orange liqueur, haunch of venison sliced (sauted in butter with garlic mushrooms, onions, tomatoes, served with red wine sauce), fresh fillet of monkfish poached in vermouth & butter (served in onion & tomato cream sauce), steak Diane, creamy spinach flaky pastry pie served with mushroom & cheese sauce.*

"This is our home, and we welcome guests into it" – Peggy and Cyril Manby treat their customers as friends, and like to chat with them. Their cosy thatched 16th century cottage is conducive of a conversational ambience, with its exposed timbers and brickwork, and soft pink and red decor. They also do their best to accommodate guests' every whim: if you don't happen to like mushrooms, they will leave them out; if you would like a particular sauce, then given the time and the right ingredients, Peggy will make it for you, but she uses only fresh produce. Such individual attention is a rare commodity, yet not injurious to the wallet, and at lunchtime (bookable Tues – Fri) a selection from the main menu is on offer at reduced prices. Wines, too, are inexpensive, and include German, French, Italian, Australian and some half-bottles.

THE RECORDERS HOUSE RESTAURANT

17 Town Street, Thaxted. Tel. (0371) 830438

Hours: 7 to 9:30pm Wed. – Sat., 12 to 2pm Wed. – Sun.
Credit cards: Access, Visa.
Price guide: A la carte £15 – £20, set price £22.50 on Saturdays.
Lunch £12.50. Light meals & coffee in rear conservatory.

Examples from menus (revised two monthly): *lobster & salmon ravioli (homemade pasta, filled with pieces of lobster & salmon mousse), pigeon breast baked encased in pastry (with bacon, chicken mousse & ginger, served on tangy blackcurrant sauce), brochette of seafood with saffron sauce (scallops, monkfish, halibut, jumbo prawns & salmon), breast of duck with lime & orange sauce. Homemade sweets, homemade icecreams & sorbets.*

In the 15th century, tax collectors were very wealthy men, if not always popular. The Recorder (as he was known) in Thaxted obviously could afford his good taste, for he had built this superb residence in the town centre, near the famed Guildhall and magnificent church and spire. Both the ground floor dining rooms enjoy views out over the main street (Thaxted is one of the region's most historic and picturesque small towns, but is only a short drive from Stansted Airport). Upstairs, another beautiful room can take private parties or wedding receptions up to 35, although a buffet for 100 is possible if using the whole restaurant. Ian Barnard is the proud owner and has lived all his life in the town, and is pleased to present an exciting Anglo-French menu to live up to the stylish surrounds. Cocktail bar, pleasant conservatory and garden. Outside catering for weddings etc welcomed.

DICKEN'S RESTAURANT

The Green, Wethersfield, nr Braintree. Tel. (0371) 850723

Hours: 7:30 to 9:30pm Tues – Sat, 12:30 to 2pm Sun. Weekday lunches by appointment only.
Credit cards: Access, Visa.
Price guide: A la carte £23, table d'hote lunch £15.

Examples from menus (revised regularly): *warm salmon tart on chive fondue, Mediterranean fish soup, rilette of duck with toasted homemade brioche; noisette of lamb on garlic & potato rosti with light basil & tomato jus, supreme of seabass meuniere on aubergine confit, roast partridge. Dark chocolate mousse with rich blackcurrant sorbet, baked apple strudel with cinammon icecream, chilled strawberry & lemon gratin.*

A new quality restaurant is always glad tidings; John Dicken acquired this, his first venture, only in October 1990, the culmination of a 20-year career. An East Anglian man, born and bred, he has garnered valuable experience in top restaurants in France and Switzerland. Inspiration for some of his dishes may have come from antiqurian cookbooks, a personal hobby. They are displayed along with 18th and 19th century cooking utensils, silverware and pewter, in this extraordinary 17th century house. Heavily timbered and oak panelled, its most unusual and engaging feature is a large minstrels gallery overlooking the dining room. John favours fresh local produce, and even has a separate 'retour de marche' menu, featuring some of the best buys on the market that day. Stylish presentation is important, but it is hearty value-for-money portions that will keep local people coming back.

THE OLD MOOT HOUSE

1 St James Street, Castle Hedingham, nr Halstead. Tel. (0787) 60342

Hours: 12 to 2pm (not Sats), 7 to 9:30pm Tues – Thurs, 7 to 10pm Fri & Sat (last orders), closed Mons.

Credit cards: Access, Visa, Diners.

Price guide: A la carte £15, set price lunch £10.75, Sun lunch £10.95 (booking essential).

Accommodation: Two Self catering cottages in village, from £100 per week, weekend breaks from £50.

Examples from menu: *to start, crab & tropical fruit hors d'oeuvre, savoury calf's liver served in Dijon mustard & cream sauce garnished with crispy bacon; to follow, medley of seafood (scallops, salmon, halibut & lemon sole poached with white wine & served with saffron & cream sauce), honey roast lamb, Forsythe steak (chargrilled sirloin topped with brown sugar & garlic butter), chicken lobster. Hot raspberry pancake with vanilla icecream, choice from trolley. Weekly specialities. Vegetaran dishes available.*

The Moot House (old English for meeting place) has been at the hub of village life for centuries, the last 12 years under the ownership of Michael and Maureen Medcraft. The beautiful timbered dining room was built as a Cross Wing Hall in 1320, making it one of the oldest inhabited dwellings in the region, but nevertheless junior to the well preserved 12th century Norman keep from which this historic village takes its name. A varied and interesting menu prepared by head chef Lez Snow, coupled with good service and popular pricing have been the key to 12 years continued success, with a well established following. An extensive wine list comprising 57 bins includes Australian, New Zealand, Californian and Chilean, and an excellent house wine at £6.50 per bottle.

RUMBLES CASTLE RESTAURANT

4 St James Street, Castle Hedingham. Tel. (0787) 61490

Hours: Dinner Tuesday – Saturday, Sunday lunch.
Credit cards: Access, Visa.
Price guide: A la carte £18, barbecue menu £12.50, Sunday lunch £12.50.

Examples from a la carte menus (revised monthly): *blue stilton mousse, Smoked tuna & smoked prawn & cream cheese terrine; goose & pigeon pie, sole & trout duet. Lychee cheesecake, Coriander egg custard. Barbecue menus (revised monthly): Pear & tarragon & stilton soup, Smoked chicken & lemon soup; Breast of duck marinated in soy sauce & garlic (chargrilled & served with teryaki sauce), Chargrilled huss with ginger & lime sauce. Jasmine tea & Cointreau icecream, Butterscotch & pecan icecream.*

Rumbles Cottage (see page 55) is now joined by this sister restaurant in historic Castle Hedingham. The "Castle" is truly an eccentric building, its narrow frontage belying an impressive interior. The back of the building is an ancient barn, with the walls leaning outwards at an alarming angle. Upstairs, the luxurious bar and coffee lounge is a forest of beams and includes a fine example of a crown pillar. Whilst the space and lavish furnishings of the "Castle" are in contrast to the more modest "Cottage", the food is very definitely in the Rumbles tradition of creativity, high quality and value for money. The a la carte menu changes in line with the "Cottage" every four weeks, but in place of the Guinea Pig menu there is a special mid-week barbecue menu of three courses and coffee for just £12.50 including VAT.

THE PULLMAN RESTAURANT

Colne Valley Railway (A604), Castle Hedingham. Tel. (0787) 62254

Hours: Brasserie 10am to 5pm Tues – Sun, 7 to 10pm Wed – Sat.
Pullman departs 7:30pm Saturday, 12:40pm Sunday.

Credit cards: Access, Visa, Amex.

Price guide: Saturdays £30 – £40. Sun lunch £18.50. Steamers Brasserie £7 – £12.

Examples from menus (revised monthly): *wild mushroom terrine sprinkled with chives, springtime salad; salmon & turbot tartar (seasoned with lime, layered with cucumber, on dill & yoghurt sauce), medallion of veal fillet on fine julienne of vegetables & foie gras (on dark veal stock with sauternes & tarragon), fillet steak in madeira sauce. Chocolate marquise on pistachio sauce, summer pudding. Full vegetarian menu. Good but simpler food at Brasserie.*

The name 'Pullman' is synonymous with luxury and high living, and there is an indefinable magic in travelling by steam train. Here is a rare opportunity to indulge in a lifestyle once exclusive to the very wealthy – the carriages were used on the royal train, the London to Paris Golden Arrow and Bournemouth Belle. But chef Mark Duggan and wife Victoria (maitre d') do not rely on novelty alone; his menus reveal verve and style, with a bucks fizz reception to set the tone. Moving gently along this pretty mile stretch of Colne Valley, one's gaze is drawn to the passing scenery, but the beautifully presented dishes are a picture in themselves. Enquire about the calendar of special evenings – could be Viennese Evening, for example, with a 30 piece orchestra on the platform. Booking is always essential, and you can even reserve the whole train for a private party! Well behaved children welcome for Sunday lunch and in brasserie.

DUNMOW'S CHINA GARDEN RESTAURANT

27 (1st floor) High Street, Gt Dunmow. Tel. (0371) 2845/5298

Hours: 12 to 2pm, 5:30 to 11:45pm. Saturday midday to midnight, Sunday 6 to 11:30pm.

Credit cards: Access, Visa, Diners, Amex.

Price guide: A la carte £12 – £18, set meals £11 – £16.50.

Examples from menu: *satay fillet steak, fried seaweed with grated scallop, deep fried crab claws stuffed with mashed prawn & crab; Szechuan aromatic duck served with pancakes, Mongolian aromatic lamb in lettuce puffs, shark's fin & vermicelli soup, iron plate sizzling chicken with ginger & spring onion, roasted pork sliced Cantonese style, steamed grey mullet in garlic & black bean sauce, fried king prawns, Mongolian hotpots.*

Do not be put off by a rather unpromising frontage; this is no ordinary Chinese restaurant. On entering, one is immediately struck by its opulence and roominess. There are three private dining areas plus the main one, in the centre of which is a fish pond. Decor is authentically Chinese, as is the cooking, but what a choice! No less than 135 dishes are listed, plus 10 chef's recommended sert dinners, including 'Gourmet Extravaganza' and Cantonese fondue (both require 24hrs notice). Few other Chinese restaurants can also offer in addition to Cantonese the superior Peking and Szechuan cuisine, and there are a number of uncommon Mongolian dishes to try. Naturally, vegetarians are also spoilt for choice. Finish your meal as the Chinese do, with the celebrated shark's fin soup, perhaps. Take away service. Large public car park to the rear.

RUMBLES COTTAGE RESTAURANT

Braintree Road, Felsted. (0371) 820996

Hours: Dinner Tuesday to Saturday, Sunday lunch.
Credit cards: Access, Visa.
Price guide: A la carte £18, 'Guinea Pig' £12.50. Sun. Lunch £12.50.

Examples from a la carte menus (revised monthly): *Smoked prawn bavarois, Creamy black olive pate; Red pepper & gruyere tagine, Duck breast Wellington. Coffee & maple syrup & pecan nut trifle, Pear & chocolate charlotte russe. Guinea Pig menus (revised 2 – 3 weeks): Mushrooms in a chilli coconut sauce, Breast of smoked chicken pan fried with scampi & served in smoked prawn sauce. Strawberry & Cointreau mousse with vanilla sauce.*

Rumbles Cottage combines the unpretentious charm of a 16th century cottage with modern British cooking, which has won national acclaim. Yet despite the quality of the cooking, you will not find it expensive. Since opening in 1983, Joy Hadley (owner and chef) has operated a policy of maintaining prices well below most other restaurants of comparable quality. In consequence this is a busy little restaurant with a large regular clientele. Of exceptionally good value, the three course Guinea Pig menu at £12.50 offers customers the opportunity on Tuesdays, Wednesdays and Thursdays to try the latest creations. Your comments will be much appreciated, and the most popular dishes graduate to the a la carte, changed every four weeks.

HUNTER'S MEET RESTAURANT

Chelmsford Road, Hatfield Heath.

Tel. (0279) 730549
Fax (0279) 731587

Hours: 16 hours 8am to midnight Tues – Fri, 7pm to midnight Sat, 12 to 5pm Sun.
Credit cards: All major cards.
Price guide: A la carte £15 – £25 (3 courses), Sunday £10.95 (4 courses).

Examples from menu: *pasta provencale, seafood pancake in veloute sauce; Dover sole, lobster Atlantis (sauted in white wine, mushrooms, topped with chef's secret sauce, flamed in brandy & topped with cheese), beef Wellington, medallions of pork flamed in brandy with creamy apricot sauce, breast of chicken stuffed with brie chives & garlic, leek & macaroni gratin, weekly specials (usually fresh fish).*

Enthusiastic new owners have made Hunter's Meet much more than just a restaurant, albeit a very spacious and well laid out one; extended hours is one important innovation: from 8am full English or champagne breakfasts are served, and morning coffees, brunches, plus ofcourse lunch and dinner. A pianist or classical guitarist plays every Thursday and Friday evening. Every third Friday of the month a full dinner dance is held, with a band and comedians, and there's also live entertainment and dancing every Saturday night. Business users have access to telephone, fax and typing facilities all day, and may meet clients (who can be collected by car) here any time. Further developments are planned, including by early 1992 a 10 bedroom extension. All this can be found just minutes from Stansted Airport, with a pleasant aspect over the famous heath. Many famous faces have become regulars, so join them and try the restaurant everyone's talking about!

THE STANSTED HARLEQUIN HOTEL

Round Coppice Road, Stansted Airport. Tel. (0279) 680800

Hours: 12 to 3pm, 6:30 to 11:30pm, 7 days.
Credit cards: All recognised cards.
Price guide: A la carte £18. Light meals from £3. Sunday lunch smorgasboard £9.95.
Accommodation: 249 rooms, 2 suites, all en suite.

Examples from menu: *tortellini ricotta with ham, smoked salmon roulade, breast of chicken poached & coated in tomato & madeira sauce, medallions of pork pan fried with marinaded mushrooms & cream, prime salmon steak coated with white wine & fresh herb sauce, chilli spiced beef, vegetable pancakes, salad bar.*

Quite unlike any other establishment featured in these pages, this newly built luxury hotel is an interesting addition to the Essex scene, and though obviously designed to meet the needs of an expanding airport, the aim is to make it the best of its kind in the area, to attract local people also. Energetic manager, Brian Stewart, was a chef and has worked in top London Hotels, so one can expect further developments and improvements to the already very considerable facilities. These include one of the finest health and leisure centres in the country, an excellent range of conference rooms, and high grade bedrooms (triple glazed, ofcourse). Despite the large size of the hotel, one should not find it impersonal, for the staff go out of their way to be friendly and helpful, and tasteful deployment of modern art and Japanese flower arrangements help create a pleasant environment.

THE PUNCH BOWL

High Easter, Chelmsford. Tel. (024 531) 222/264

Hours: Open for dinner (last orders 9:45pm). Closed Sunday evenings & Mondays. Lunch by arrangement.

Credit cards: Access, Visa, Diners, Amex.

Price guide: A la carte £17, midweek menu £15.90, Sun. lunch £12.90.

Examples from menus (revised seasonally): *mousseline of chicken with pistachio nuts & melba toast, deep fried mushrooms with garlic mayonnaise, Norfolk samphire; goujons of sole with almonds, walnut casserole, rack of English lamb, fresh breast of Thaxted duck with blackberry coulis, calves liver with bacon & raisins. Mrs Wright's butterscotch tart & other homemade puddings & savouries.*

David Kelsey and his dynamic band of colleagues have built this into one of the most reliable and popular restaurants in the area (early booking advised!). It can have done no harm to be in an appealing 15th century house (next to church) in a pleasant little village with an odd name. At the reception bar you'll find yourself standing on a lovely solid willow floor, and the roomy restaurant has its full complement of exposed timbers – ideal for beautiful weddings and small functions (larger ones in the marquee). But attention to fresh food is the key; fish from Billingsgate, local vegetables and home grown herbs, for example. All soups, sauces and desserts are homemade. Set price menus are very good value, and a well above average wine list numbers over 200. Outside catering a speciality.

THE FARMHOUSE FEAST

The Street, Roxwell, nr Chelmsford. Tel. (0245) 248583

Hours: 7 to 9:30pm Tues – Sat. Lunches by reservation.
Credit cards: Not accepted.
Price guide: £21 (5 courses). 3 courses £16 (Tues – Thurs only). Lunch £8.50 (2 courses), £12.50 (3 courses).

Examples from menus (revised weekly): *filo parcel filled with butter beans (cooked with leeks & celery, served with barbecue sauce), mint pancakes (filled with goats cheese, apple & millet, baked with mushroom sauce); pieces of chicken marinated with yoghurt & spices (served with brown rice & homemade fig chutney), steak & kidney pie, pork escalopes baked with tomato sauce & topped with mozarella, boned trout with light orange & ginger sauce. Pavlova, bread & butter pudding.*

Healthy eating is very much at the heart of chef proprietor Rosemary Upson's approach; half the menu is vegetarian, organic and wholefoods are used whenever possible, and everything is homemade, even the bread, cream cheese and petits fours. For extra interest the last Friday of each month is 'gourmet evening', an opportunity to try very special cuisines from Mexico, Denmark, the Caribbean or almost anywhere else, and red letter days like Valentine's and Beaujolais are also well observed. Whichever, there's always a good vegetarian choice, for Rosemary is herself vegetarian. She's been here since 1982, having started with outside catering (still going strong), and has secured a regular place in major good food guides. No smoking area, and rooms available for private parties.

NEIL'S RESTAURANT

142 High Street, Epping. Tel. (0378) 76767
NB From Feb '92 tel. no. will be (0992) 576767

Hours: 12 to 2pm, 6:30 to 10pm Wed – Sun. Closed Mon & Tues.
Credit cards: Visa, Amex.
Price guide: A la carte set price £19.50 (2 courses), £23.50 (3 courses). Table d'hote £12.65 (2 courses), £16 (3 courses). Lunchtime £5 for 2 courses.

Examples from menus (revised three weekly): *warm seafood salad (incl. clams, tiger prawns, baby squid, French seaweed), Epping Forest wild mushroom ceps served in homemade brioche; baked red snapper (stuffed with squid & crab, served on saffron champagne sauce), noisette of spring lamb with blackcurrant & port sauce with leek & shallot timbale, trio of wild Epping game (partridge, duck & pheasant) served with spiced cabbage & sherry sauce. Hot souffle of the day (eg passion fruit with mango sorbet – see photo), trio of chocolate mousses served with trio of chocolate sauces (white, milk & bitter). Excellent cheeseboard of 25 varieties.*

Proprietor Neil Cohen has never worked in less than a two star Michelin restaurant, and he is en route to earning his own at this exciting newcomer to the Essex scene. Still only in his mid-twenties, his enthusiasm will clearly take him a long way, and his commitment to quality and freshness borders on the extreme – he has game shot locally, to be delivered within an hour, and even catches his own trout! Yet he is no 'food snob', and will, if asked, prepare a well done steak. Indeed, any special requests, such as obtaining a certain wine, will be accommodated if possible. His approachability and flexibilty have wone many converts, and he knows most of his customers by name. His unpredictable menus cater for all palates, but dishes are always presented with style – "Art on a plate" as Neil describes it.

THE SHOES RESTAURANT

The Street; High Ongar. Tel. (0277) 363350

Hours: 12 to 2:30pm & 7 to 9:45pm Mon – Fri, 7 to 9:45pm Sat, 12 to 2:30pm Sun.

Credit cards: Access, Visa.

Price guide: A la carte £22, lunch £16 – £25. Sun lunch £12.95.

Examples from menus (revised daily): *roast lamb sweetbreads (with pine nut, French bean & raspberry salad), salmon & langoustine ravioli in coriander sauce; venison on rosti with port sauce & blueberries, supreme of chicken stuffed with parma ham served on tarragon sauce with sauteed polenta, steamed fillets of plaice with filo pastry 'pan' filled with petit ratatouille & garlic jus. Iced poppyseed parfait with fresh raspberries & kirsch sauce, hot passion fruit & Grand Marnier souffle.*

"We don't have daily specials – everything is special every day" – not a conceit, but the mark of one who trained at Claridges, Harrods and Corney & Barrow. Proprietor Lyndon Wootton has made this beautiful 16th century coaching inn a restaurant of the highest calibre by never compromising standards. Head chef Paul Spry (ex Reform Club, Hyatt Carlton, Inigo Jones) and his talented 'brigade' use only the freshest ingredients in creating exciting dishes, as pleasing to the eye as to the palate. Even bread and pasta are homemade. Aperitifs and cocktails are served in two lounge areas, or in the garden (with marquee for weddings etc) in summer. The restaurant seats 58 in style – starched linen, crystal glasses and fresh flowers – and the table is yours for the evening. An upstairs dining room seats 24 and is perfect for private parties. The 'Express' business lunch is guaranteed to be just that, or a 50% refund. Good wine list, many in half bottles.

THE ITALIAN ROOM AT THE KING'S HEAD

1 Church Hill, Loughton. Tel. (081 508) 1167

Hours: 6 to 10:30 pm, 7 days. Bar meals 11am to 3pm, 7 days.
Credit cards: Access, Visa.
Price guide: A la carte £18. Sun lunch £9.95. 12½% service charge. Bar snacks from £1.15.

Examples from menu (incl. many weekly specials): *homecured gravadlax with avocado mousse & crab, tenerelli deliziosi (pancake with soft cheese, spinach, herbs), pizzas, sogliola Veneziana (fillets of sole with lobster, salmon, dill & caviar sauce), veal piccata in lemon sauce, stuffed rolled steak in paprika sauce, monkfish pizzaiola, supreme of duck or chicken. With 24hrs notice:– bouillabesse, paella, suckling pig. Sweet trolley.*

It is not always easy to establish a high class restaurant under the same roof as a traditional informal pub. It has been successfully achieved here by defining the 80–seater restaurant with a quite separate, Italian identity. A little piece of the Mediterranean has been carved out in the unlikely setting of Loughton, by felicitous deployment of Italian background music, pictures of Italian scenes, whirring ceiling fans, luxurious furnishings and, most important, Italian cooking of a very high order. It is depressingly common for the English to assume Italian food is just pizza and pasta, but it was one of the world's great cuisines long before the French entered the scene. On the enormous menu you will find many well known classics as well as speciality dishes, some exotic others remarkably simple, but all very tasty.

THE SPOTTED DOG

Ivy Chimneys, Ivy Chimneys Road, Epping. Tel. (0378) 72612

Hours: 7 to 10:30pm (not Mon). Bar meals lunch & evening Mon – Sat.

Credit cards: Access, Visa.

Price guide: A la carte £16. Sunday lunch £9.95 (children £4.95). Bar snacks from £1.15.

Examples from menu: *julienne of mixed vegetables & nuts served in chablis vinaigrette, mussels black velvet (with onion, Guinness, champagne & cream sauce), tagliatelle van homrigh (with fresh & smoked salmon in light cream & garlic sauce); fillet of pork Vanessa (stuffed with potato filling, wrapped in bacon, roasted & served in white wine & mushroom sauce), guinea fowl stuffed with guinea fowl & cashewnut mousse (with black cherry & apple sauce), strips of salmon & monkfish weaved into a trellice (poached & served with light dill sauce), vegetarian parcels. Homemade sweets.*

A very popular pub (featured in our last 'Best Inns & Pubs' guide), the Spotted Dog also has a restaurant which stands on its own merits. The cool mint dining room seats 50 in comfort, after an extensive (and expensive!) refit. Versatile Irish chef Gerry Gillen presents a large and balanced menu, using fresh ingredients, which includes some traditional favourites, like beef Wellington or rack of lamb en croute, with some interesting creations like veal Baileys. Eating out should be fun, and many party nights are organised, such as Guy Fawkes, 'Rocky Horror' or Christmas. Private functions (up to 45) are also well catered for. Incidentally, the King's Head in Loughton is under the same management. Booking advised.

LITTLE HAMMONDS

51 High Street, Ingatestone. Tel.(0277) 353194

Hours: 12 to 2:30pm, 6 to 11pm 7 days.
Credit cards: Access, Visa, Switch.
Price guide: A la carte £22.50 set price. Set lunch £8.75 Mon – Fri, set dinner £13.95 Mon – Fri.

Examples from menus (revised quarterly, plus daily specials): *fish sausage with chives (served with chervil sauce), ravioli ratatouille (with julienne of vegetables & roquefort sauce), mushroom tartlet (assorted mushrooms kissed with garlic, finished with white wine cream sauce); Strawberry sherbet (sorbet with compote of strawberries, served on strawberry coulis); duck Whadden Chase (supreme pierced with rosemary on bed of apricot stuffing, finished with hint of garlic, shallot white wine, beef glace, jus-lie). Vegetarian dishes.*

Proprietor Stuart Hammond acquired his expertise at various high class hotels and restaurants, and opened here in August 1987. The 'little' refers to the cottage in which it is housed, which dates from 1558 (the history is described on the front of the menu), and is as charming as one could hope for. The old A12 has been bypassed, leaving the village to slumber peacefully, and sparing the ancient beams from the juggernauts. Head chef Mark Jeans offers several 'creations' (named after local villages) in a style that is a combination of the best new ideas in cooking, with French, classical and nouvelle cuisine ('nouvelle' being only in the garnish, not size of portions!). The 'Rose Room' is available for private parties up to 18, and Stuart also runs a very professional outside catering service (tel. 352927) for all kinds of events. If the delicious aroma of fresh baked bread wafts around you, that will be from his bakehouse next door!

THE DUKE OF YORK

Southend Road, Billericay (A 129) Tel. (0277) 651403

Hours: Lunctime & evening every day, except Saturday lunch & all day Sunday.

Credit cards: Access, Visa, Diners, Amex.

Price guide: A la carte (now also in French & German) £20 – £25. Table d'hote £15.75. Bar meals.

Examples from menus (revised quarterly, specials vary daily): *crab claws in garlic butter & cream, smoked eel in garlic butter, homemade soups; fillet of salmon in crab & mussel sauce, monkfish in prawn & mornay sauce, strips of veal in French mustard sauce, chicken supreme in tandoori & cream sauce, strips of fillet steak in dill & coriander sauce, spinach & tomato roulade with hollandaise sauce, grills. Crepes Suzettes, homemade sweets & gateaux.*

Even though the menus are enormous, pride is taken in the freshness of all ingredients. Fish, for example, is delivered daily from the London markets, and all the sweets and gateaux are made on the premises. Chef Terry Parkin specialises in delicious sauces of all kinds, but will cook any dish to customer requirements. Those who prefer their food simple and without adornment have a wide choice of grilled meats and fish, and vegetarians have their own separate menu. Over 120 wines from all over the world are listed with helpful descriptions, and staff are all well trained in the subject (often overlooked elsewhere). An outstanding selection of malt whiskies would delight even the most discerning Scot. Built as an inn in 1801, The Duke of York is still a lively and popular pub, but the bright, attractive restaurant is quite separate. The antique cash register (in £. s. d.) will stir a little nostalgia!

EDELWEISS SWISS RESTAURANT

1613 London Road, Leigh-on-Sea. Tel. (0702) 711517

Hours: 7 to 10pm, Mon. – Sat. Private lunches by arrangement.
Credit cards: Access, Visa.
Price guide: A la carte £18 – £20 (incl. drink).

Examples from menus (specials vary daily): *Swiss veal sausage served with sauerkraut & potato salad, Swiss noodles (with ham, olives, tuna fish, oregano, garlic & cream), vegetable croquette; fillet of venison & veal (roasted with whisky sauce, served with cranberries & chestnut puree), roasted chicken breast fillet with Gruyere cheese & Swiss ham (with brandy & white wine in cream sauce), fillets of sole stuffed with mussels (rolled in smoked salmon, poached in white wine with sauce Allemande), vegetarian dishes, flambes, fondues. Sweets & savouries.*

From land-locked mountainous Switzerland to the flat Essex coast – the contrast could hardly be starker, but chef proprietor Herbert Staudhammer has successfully recreated a little piece of that country here over the past 11 years. His career began in Zurich, garnering further experience from Germany, Paris and at the German Food Centre in Knightsbridge. These influences are evident from his varied and mouthwatering Franco-Germanic menus (only freshest ingredients), though he will be pleased to meet special requests if given sufficient notice – steak & kidney pudding and spotted dick are recent examples! The cosy restaurant seats just 40, but there's only one sitting, so one may relax and perhaps share a fondue, a most sociable way of eating, accompanied perhaps by one of 14 uncommon Swiss wines.

BAUMANN'S BRASSERIE

4 – 6 Stoneham Street, Coggeshall. Tel. (0376) 561453
Hours: 7:30 to 10pm, Tues. – Sat. 12:30 to 2pm, Tues. – Sun.
Credit cards: All major cards.
Price guide: A la carte £15 – £20. Special daily business lunch £9.95.

Examples from menus (revised monthly): *wild boar terrine with grenadine caramelised onion marmalade, English stilton & port mousse (with compote of diced apples, celery & onions), cold poached Mediterranean fish flaked in subtle dressing; seared sirloin steak with creamy tarragon sauce, poached lobster & monkfish collops in nage of shredded vegetables, baked breast of Pere Gaston duck in tangy orange juices, Billingsgate catch of the day. Rich dark chocolate truffle cake with crushed raspberry coulis, hot rum souffle, summer pudding.*

One of England's most attractive small towns, Coggeshall enjoys a rural location some seven miles from Colchester and close to Braintree and Chelmsford. It is noted for having 15 antique shops and many fine listed buildings, among them 16th century Baumann's Brasserie, owned by Mark Baumann and Doug Wright. Young and enthusiastic, they learned their culinary skills in some of the most reputable restaurants in this country and France. Only fresh food is used, and all dishes are cooked to order, whether chosen from the a la carte (revised monthly), or the popular business lunches (served weekdays). Well worth considering as a venue for a wedding reception or private party – up to 80 people can be seated.

LE TALBOOTH RESTAURANT

Gun Hill, Dedham, nr Colchester. Tel. (0206) 323150

Hours: 12 to 2pm, 7 to 9pm, 7 days.
Credit cards: Access, Visa.
Price guide: A la carte £32, table d'hote lunches £18.50.
Accommodation: 10 suites at nearby Maison Talbooth (transport provided).

Examples from menus (revised two monthly, plus daily specials): *mousseline of langoustines (filled with crab and enhanced with a delicate champagne & caviar sauce), quail filled with a chicken & herb mousseline; roasted pigeon with ravioli of livers and essence of truffle & ceps, roulade of sole (enhanced with a carrot, ginger & coriander butter), Scottish beef (bound in wild mushroom mousseline, with shallots, garlic and rich Burgundy wine sauce). Tartlet of bananas (served on amaretto sauce, surrounded by flaked almonds), mille feuille of white chocolate mousse (enhanced with macerated raisins & sultanas, on pool of vanilla sauce).*

One of the most celebrated restaurants in the region, even the country, Le Talbooth is rated highly by all the major guides, and amongst many accolades boasts two Egon Ronay stars, the AA rosette and Ackerman Clover Award for culinary excellence. The wine list, too, is universally commended. If this were not enough, it is one of our loveliest buildings, and enjoys a wonderful position on the banks of the river Stour – Constable country. It has been the source of many distinguished chefs, though head chef Steven Blake came from Le Meridien, Piccadilly. Nearby is the luxurious **Maison Talbooth** with 10 magnificent suites, and also under the same ownership is the charming **Dedham Vale Hotel** and **Terrace Restaurant** (tel. 0206 322273), and at Harwich a well reputed seafood restaurant, the **Pier** (tel. 0255 241212). It all began nearly 40 years ago for proprietor Gerald Milsom, and now son David is managing director.

THE ANGEL INN

Stoke by Nayland, nr Colchester. Tel. (0206) 263245

Hours: 12:30 to 1:30pm, Wed – Sun. 7:30 to 9pm (last orders) Tues – Sat. Bar meals lunch & evening, 7 days.
Credit cards: Access, Visa, Diners, Amex.
Price guide: A la carte £20, bar £10.50, Sun lunch £10.50.
Accommodation: 5 doubles, 1 twin, all en suite.

Examples from ever changing menus: *chilled melon with ginger & mango coulis, gratin of seafoods baked in cream & white wine sauce under a crisp garlic topping, terrine of Suffolk chicken on light yoghurt dressing flavoured with lime; Suffolk beef pie, supreme of local pheasant on foaming sherry sauce, baked salmon mousse en croute on cream & dill sauce, fresh lobster, fresh local fish & exotic (flown in), vegetarian dish.*

In the heart of Constable country, this lovely village is blessed with one of the most admired inns of the region, a stalwart of most of the main good food guides, possessing a lively, bustling bar and first rank restaurant. The street frontage is Georgian, but as the rear view above suggests, origins are 17th century. This is more evident inside; the timbered dining room is superb, and overlooked by a gallery, which leads to six very well appointed bedrooms. Many customers travel a fair distance for the atmosphere and chef Mark Johnson's cooking; he manages an astonishing twice daily change of bar menu, yet does not compromise on the quality or freshness of the produce, nor the stylish presentation. Fresh fish is a speciality, always available, and may be simply griddled, if preferred. Owners Richard Wright and Peter Smith always recommend booking ahead.

THE FRIARS RESTAURANT & BUSINESS CENTRE

17 Friars Street, Sudbury. Tel. (0787) 72940

Hours: Breakfast, morning coffee, lunch, afternoon teas, dinner Mon – Sat & Sun lunch (free entry to Gainsborough's House).
Credit cards: Access, Visa, Diners, Amex.
Price guide: A la carte £15 – £20, table d'hote £7.35 (served all day).
Accommodation: 1 single £17.50, 1 double £25. Tv's, tea & coffee.

Examples from menus (revised regularly): *wild mushrooms in puff pastry with Noilly cream sauce, port & stilton mousse, spinach timbales; paupiettes of sole filled with crab & ginger, noisettes of lamb with mushroom sauce & courgette gateau, fresh salmon in puff pastry with dill Vermouth sauce. Frozen cream mousse with red fruits, white & dark chocolate marquise, apricot omelet, cheeses.*

Once the Weavers' Guildhall, this superb 15th century timbered building is now again used as a business meeting centre, as well as a top class French and English restaurant. The first of the two beautiful air-conditioned dining rooms has a marvellous inglenook, the second a unique original window overlooking a courtyard garden. The upstairs Guild Room, long and light, provides the atmosphere required for working seminars or entertainment. Chef owner Anne Mary Robinson, trained in a Michelin star Paris restaurant, has secured a place in the Michelin and other good food guides with classic French cuisine supplemented by monthly regional menus from all over the world. Gourmet evenings, wine tastings, cookery demonstrations – the mailing list has details. Off-street parking can be reserved evenings and weekends. Courtesy car by arrangement. Member of 'Two for One' dining club. Full range of outside catering, including Champagne Breakfast in Bed delivered to the home by butler or chambermaid!

THE BELL HOTEL

Market Hill, Clare. Tel. (0787) 277741

Hours: 12 to 2:30pm, 7 to 9:30pm daily.
Credit cards: Access, Visa, Diners, Amex.
Price guide: A la carte £19, table d'hote £14.50, lunch £7.50.
Accommodation: 20 romms, most en suite, with tv's, telephones. Some with 4-posters, Clare Suite has whirlpool.

Examples from menu: *quails eggs with smoked bacon & crispy croutons on bed of crisp green leaves, char grilled sardines in rich tomato sauce; fresh salmon baked in pastry case on bed of rich brandy & lobster sauce, large magret duck breast with pocket of raspberries on sharp raspberry sauce, fillet of pork en croute (stuffed with apricots, served with light apricot & schnapps sauce), breast of chicken filled with ham mousse & carved on to creamy cheese sauce, steaks, vegetable & nut curry, chef's daily specials.*

The Bell is synonymous with Clare (one of Suffolk's prettiest small towns), and the two have been together since the 16th century. Its beautiful interior blends modern comforts with unspoilt period charm. A recent addition has been a pleasant conservatory to the rear, where one can enjoy aperitifs or after dinner coffee. Afternoon teas in the lounge are a favourite with the ladies, but it is the first class restaurant which commands most respect. Chef Gavin Bennetto's menus will revive the most jaded palate, complemented by an extensive wine list. (For simpler bistro meals try Leggers next door). With two function suites, The Bell is well able to cater for weddings, conferences etc. The Miles family also now owns The George at Ramsey.

BARRETTS RESTAURANT

31 Egremont Street, Glemsford, nr Sudbury Tel. (0787) 281573
NB Barretts is due to move in Dec '91, and will be known as THE SCUTCHERS, Westgate Street, Long Melford. Tel. (0787) 310200. Food will be as good, served in Brasserie style.

Hours: Open for lunch & dinner Tues. – Sat. and Sunday lunch and Dinner
Credit cards: Access, Visa.
Price guide: Set £19.95 (two courses), £24.95 (three), £29.50 (four). Sun. lunch £13.95.

Examples from menus (revised monthly): *roast rabbit in puff pastry case with jus of basil, mushroom consomme topped with light curry sabayon; navarin of sea fish with pasta rosti & red wine sauce, strips of beef with a soy & ginger sauce (with 'tagliatelle' of vegetables), breast of duck with rich cassis sauce. White chocolate sorbet & bitter chocolate parfait with confit of kumquats, roast pears with honey & ginger icecream, selection of British cheeses.*

"Never judge a book by its covers" – a particularly apt maxim, for behind the uninspiring Victorian shopfront you'll find a pleasant lounge and dining room, small but not crowded, cosy but not twee. Almost as important as the good food is the friendly, courteous service that is the stamp of family run restaurants. Diane Barrett receives guests while husband Nicholas, trained at top restaurants, prepares dishes of originality and diversity from the freshest of ingredients. Each course offers from four to six alternatives. The major food guides have all been quick to recognise his talent, which has also gained the attention of national newspapers, and the rare and prestigious red 'M' from Michelin. Outside catering is a speciality (trading under the name "At home with Barretts"), for any occasion from a private dinner party to a wedding or business function.

THE COUNTRYMEN RESTAURANT AT THE BLACK LION HOTEL

The Green, Long Melford. Tel. (0787) 79951 –restnt (0787) 312356 –hotel
Fax (0787) 74557

Hours:	Open for lunch & dinner (last orders 9:30pm). Closed Sunday & Monday evenings. Morning coffee, afternoon tea.
Credit cards:	Access, Visa.
Price guide:	Set price from £17.50 (4 courses plus coffee & hand made chocs). Lunch set price £10.50 (3 courses plus tea or coffee).
Accommodation:	10 doubles/twins, all en suite from £40 single, £60 double. Suite £80.

Examples from menus (revised monthly): *marbled tomato & avocado mousse with crabmeat mayonnaise, spinach & ricotta cheese ravioli (in bacon, tomato & fresh basil sauce); quenelles of sole in crayfish & tomato sauce, prime fillet steak stuffed with pate (wrapped in bacon, served in port wine sauce), julienne of veal in mushroom & cheese sauce, lentil & mushroom lasagne. Homemade sweets & chocolates.*

Long Melford is a lovely village, England's longest and a Mecca for antique collectors, with arguably the finest parish church in the land. Standing right on the green, very close to the church, this handsome 17th century coaching inn commands lovely views over the village from some of the roomy bedrooms (currently being refurbished). Dorchester trained Stephen Errington continues to present two imaginative menus at both lunch and dinner, of a standard to maintain the hard won place in major guides. Wife Janet takes care of the hospitality side, and is also an expert on the 150 wines on an outstanding list. The cheeseboard is something of a speciality, and there are over 100 liqueurs from which to choose. An outstanding location for business and/or pleasure, and having two rooms for meetings up to 30 – ask about business packages.

THE SWAN HOTEL

High Street, Lavenham. Tel. (0787) 247477

Hours: 12:30 to 2pm, 7 to 9:30pm, 7 days.
Credit cards: Access, Visa, Diners, Amex, Forte Gold Card.
Price guide: A la carte £30. Table d'hote £18.95. Lunch £12.95.
Accommodation: 47 bedrooms, all en suite, including 2 suites and 2 four posters.

Examples from menus (revised seasonally): *rilletes of goose with toasted brioche, medley of seafood & ratatouille; braised fillet of brill & fettuccini (simmered in vermouth), breast of pheasant & apple mille feuille, fillet of English lamb with apricot & lemon farce, fillet steak & woodland mushrooms, Covent Garden tart, vegetable bake in mild curry sauce with toasted almonds.*

Even amongst East Anglia's rich legacy of splendid architecture, the 14th century Swan is especially admired, in the perfect setting of England's best preserved small town. The interior invariably stirs the imagination of all who see it; stout oak beams and lintelled fireplaces on a grand scale, and in the restaurant high timbered ceiling and minstrels gallery. But The Swan is equally feted by gourmets. Small portions may be requested by diners who wish to create their own gastronomic menu, and head chef Andrew Barrass offers in addition his own carefully chosen 'Signature Menu'. In such elegant surrounds, accompanied by Peter on the piano, the management's request that gentlemen wear jacket and tie for dinner does not seem unreasonable. A memorable place to stay, and highly rated by most major guides.

BRADFIELD HOUSE RESTAURANT & HOTEL

Bradfield Combust, nr. Bury St. Edmunds. Tel. (0284) 386301

Restnt hours: 7 to 9pm Wed. – Sat., plus Sun. lunch (12 to 1:45pm).
Credit cards: Access, Visa.
Price guide: A la carte £14.50, table d'hote £12.50. Sun. lunch £11.50
Accommodation: 4 large en suite bedrooms, with full facilities, from £40 single to £55 double.

Examples from menus (revised 6 weekly): *creamy cauliflower & stilton soup, duck breast salad, hot prawn souffle, hotpot of garnished mushrooms with cream sauce & puff pastry lid; fillet of beef rolled in crushed black peppercorns & garlic (flamed in brandy & served in slices), scallop of salmon with fresh orange & ginger, individual pies of venison & game (speciality), roast rack of lamb with caramelised onions. Homemade desserts.*

Overlooking the small village green is the characteristic pink-wash and timbered facade of 17th century Bradfield House. Inside, antique furniture and fireplaces, old French woodburning stoves, parlour palms, art deco lamps and colourful pictures and furnishings combine most effectively to create a warm and pleasant atmosphere. It is all insulated by two acres of beautiful Victorian gardens, including a kitchen herb garden – chef proprietor Roy Ghijben takes great pride in using only the freshest of ingredients. He and wife Sally came here only two years or so ago, but their style of traditional English combined with rural French has quickly got the attention of major guides – no surprise to those who knew them at Weavers, Hadleigh. They keep a fine wine cellar, and the bedrooms are of a high standard. Private meeting room and business lunches by arrangement.

THE FOUR HORSESHOES

Wickham Road, Thornham Magna, nr Eye. Tel. (037 971) 777

Hours: 12 to 2:30pm, 7:30 to 9:30pm.
Credit cards: Access, Visa, Diners, Amex.
Price guide: A la carte from £20.
Accommodation: 5 doubles, 1 family, 2 singles, all en suite. Weekend breaks £110 (b & b + dinner, 2 people for 2 nights).

Examples from menus (revised regularly): *fresh fish, well hung steaks, guinea fowl forestiere, fresh lobster in season, vegetarian choice. Trad. Sun lunch. Bar: homebaked honey ham, homemade pies, vegetable & nut cutlets, ploughman's, daily specials.*

Bar

Restaurant

The Four Horseshoes
Country Inn and Hotel

One of East Anglia's best known hostelries, 'The Shoes' always bustles with life. As the watercolour suggests, it is the archetypal dream thatched cottage, a delight on the eye both inside and out. The massive low beams and mud and daub walls indicate great age – over 800 years, in fact. Foreign visitors, especially those from 'the New World', are open mouthed at such well preserved antiquity. We natives are more blase, being more concerned with the abundance of good food from a wide choice, in both bar and restaurant. The new management took over in the summer of 1990.

The bedrooms are luxurious, and residents have their own lounge. Dogs are permitted by arrangement (not in restaurant or bar), and well behaved children are welcome – cots are provided for the very young. This is a lovely area to explore: nearby Thornham Park is full of wild deer and rare orchids, ideal for a quite stroll. There are water meadows with kingfishers and kestrels, and Thornham Parva church is worth seeing for its uncommon mediaeval wall paintings and thatched roof. One is also well placed to travel further afield: north to Norwich and the Broads, east to the coast, south to Ipswich and Constable Country, and west to Bury St Edmunds, Newmarket and Cambridge.

THE OLD COUNTING HOUSE RESTAURANT

Haughley, nr. Stowmarket. Tel. (0449) 673617

Hours: From 12 noon Mon. – Fri. and from 7:30pm Mon. – Sat.
Credit cards: Access, Visa.
Price guide: Table d'hote dinner £17.50 (4 courses). Lunch £11 (snacks £4)

Examples from menus (revised three weekly): *garlic stuffed mussels, winter salad (warm chicken livers in orange dressing), baked avocado filled with herb pate; duck scallopine (breast thinly sliced with a honey, lemon, raisin & white rum glaze), poached salmon topped with buttery fennel sauce. Caramelled oranges with whisky, apricot & almond vacherin, chocolate & Tia Maria mousse. Savoury – Austrian Beignets (deep fried smoked cheese). Lunchtime snacks – prawns in cheese sauce with crispy topping, served with granary rolls & salad bowl).*

Once a bank (hence the name), the long and chequered history of this marvellous old building goes back to the 13th century, the original still in tact. Custodians of this long history are Paul and Susan Woods (who cooks). In the best tradition of family run concerns, one is assured of that personal touch which can make such a difference to the enjoyment of a meal, and ofcourse all is absolutely fresh and homecooked. The set price menu is exceptionally good value for four courses, and there are six choices of starters and main course, plus a sweet trolley. The list of 56 wines includes Australian, New Zealand and Potuguese (try excellent value 1980 Garrafeira red). Why not pamper yourself a little and call in for lunch? The fare is lighter and is certainly not expensive. Les Routiers and AA recommended. Ample parking on quiet road.

TOT HILL HOUSE RESTAURANT

Bury Road, nr. Stowmarket. Tel. (0449) 673375
(on A45 at Fishpond Way junction)

Hours: 7 to 9:30pm, Tues. – Sat. Sun. lunch 12 to 2pm.
Credit cards: Access, Visa, Mastercard, Eurocard.
Price guide: A la carte from £16. Gourmet menu £14.75 (4 courses & coffee) Sunday lunch £8.50.

Examples from menus (a la carte revised occasionally, gourmet 5 weekly): *mussels thermidor, pineapple surprise (fans of pineapple with chive and lime cream cheese garnished with prawns), seafood platter; beef Chinese style, Rabbit Somerset (in cider, cream, apples and sage), poached fillet of bream laced with lobster and prawn sauce, poussin Jamaican style, fillet en croute, magret duck, Barnsley lamb chop, sea bass (baked in cream, mussels, prawns and white wine), all with fresh veg. Homemade sweets.*

More than 13 years experience lies behind the ever widening reputation of this relative newcomer to the region. Chef Andrew McBain has been pleasing palates for that long but, with parents John and Jean, opened here only in the spring of '88. First they had to completely renovate this striking 16th century farmhouse, standing in two acres of garden on a hilltop by the eastbound carriageway of the A45. The exterior is lined with woolpit brick, as used on The White House, Washington. The food, too, is fit for a president; the gourmet menu is exceptionally good value, the vegetables absolutely fresh, and the sweets irresistable. Three house wines are backed by a list of around 40 supplied by Lay & Wheeler. An excellent venue for private parties (up to 40 seated, 50 buffet) and ofcourse wedding receptions etc. Unusually, there are full facilities for the disabled.

CLAYDON COUNTRY HOUSE HOTEL & RESTAURANT

Ipswich Road, Claydon. Tel. (0473) 830382

Hours: Lunch 12:00 onwards, dinner 7 to 10pm, 7 days.
Credit cards: Access, Visa, Diners, Amex.
Price guide: A la carte £20.
Accommodation: 14 rooms en suite, some four-posters. From £49 single, £69 double, £79 family. Weekend breaks (2 nights dinner, bed & breakfast) £128 for two, inclusive.

Examples from menus (revised seasonally): *flakes of fresh salmon wrapped in sweet sponge with cordon of tomato coulis & sevruga caviar, homemade ravioli stuffed with shellfish mousseline bathed in dill & saffron scented beurre blanc sauce; apricot sorbet; breast of chicken (filled with a chestnut, almond & kumquat farce, finished with orange piquant sauce), duo of salmon & sole on bed of crispy noodles with creamy champagne sauce, vegetable stroganoff. Layers of crisp dark chocolate & white chocolate mousse surrounded by fruit coulis, sweet open pancakes filled with roasted fruits flamed in kirsch.*

Better viewed from the landscaped gardens than the road, this is a warm and sumptuously appointed country house in the best English tradition, now under new ownership. Bedrooms are individually designed, and each has excellent facilities. The regency style restaurant enjoys a first class reputation (booking advised), and draws on the best from local butchery and market garden. Although peacefully situated in a small village, the hotel is just a few hundred yards from the A45, and very handy for Ipswich and Felixstowe to the east, and Cambridge and Bury St. Edmunds to the west. Weekend breaks are good value.

HINTLESHAM HALL

Hintlesham, nr Ipswich. Tel. (047 387) 334/268

Hours: Open for lunch & dinner (last orders 9:45pm).
Closed Saturday lunchtime except by arrangement.
Credit cards: Access, Visa, Diners, Amex.
Price guide: Fixed price a la carte £29.50 (3 courses Sun. – Thurs.), £37.50 (4 courses Fri./Sat.). Lunch £18.50.
Accommodation: 33 rooms (incl. 5 suites) all en suite, from £85 to £300.

Examples from menus (revised seasonally): *saffron ravioli (filled with langoustines, sun dried tomatoes & peppers set on a light shellfish sauce); quail surrounded by its own farce & wrapped in puff pastry served with Madeira sauce; supreme of Norfolk guinea fowl cooked in its own juices set on basil flavoured noodles & dark port sauce. Honey & pistachio nougatine glace with tuile biscuit curls & coffee bean sauce, light raspberry mousse resting on lime parfait surrounded by its own coulis.*

One of our most distinguished country houses, Hintlesham is celebrated nationally and even internationally. Behind the 18th century facade the original Tudor building stands in all its glory. The Salon dining room, once a ballroom, is exquisite, grand without being too imposing, and the panelled Parlour dining room, is also delightful. In fact, all the rooms are magnificent and sumptuously furnished, but most important, perhaps, is the kitchen. Chef Alan Ford (ex Dorchester) and his team enjoy a reputation for excellence to match the elegant surroundings. Hone the appetite with a stroll around the lovely gardens, or for the more sporting clay pigeon shooting or fishing can be arranged, and a new 18 hole golf course provides further diversion to go with the existing billiards, tennis and croquet.

KWOK'S RENDEZVOUS

23 St. Nicholas Street, Ipswich. Tel. (0473) 256833
Hours: Lunch & dinner Mon. – Sat. Closed bank hols.
Credit cards: Amex, Diners.

Examples from menus: *Szechuen sliced pork (on bed of pickled salad with chilli & garlic sauce), sweet & sour wan-tun, prawn with sesame; five willows sole (crisp fried in sweet & sour sauce), aromatic & crispy duck, Peking beef fillet (sauteed with fruity bean sauce), quick fried lamb with spring onion, chicken in black bean sauce, lotus root sauteed with hot bean paste.*

Listed among the top 20 Chinese restaurants in the U.K. by The Sunday Express, in the top 10 by American Express, and in a major good food guide since 1984, clearly this is no run-of-the-mill Chinese, and it enjoys the respect of restaurateurs of all kinds in the area. Most important, the public loves it and have been flocking here for over 10 years. That's how long Thomas Kwok has been presenting his mainly Peking, plus Szechuen and Hunan dishes, recognised as the elite of Chinese cooking. Mrs Kwok takes care of front of house, aided by smart, mostly English young waiters (no language problem!). Also untypical is the decor, subdued and tasteful, as one would expect of a first rate establishment. A bit tricky to find (opp. Cromwell Square), but near the town centre and a car park, and well worth seeking out.

THE WAVERLEY HOTEL & WOLSEY RESTAURANT

Wolsey Gardens, Felixstowe. Tel. (0394) 282811 Fax (0394) 670185
Telex 987568 WAVLEY G.

Hours: Lunch 12:00 onwards, dinner 7 to 10pm, 7 days.
Credit cards: Access, Visa, Diners, Amex.
Price guide: A la carte £13 – £15. Bar meals from £2.50.
Accommodation: 20 rooms, all en suite. From £44.50 single, £61.25 double, £65 family. Weekend breaks (2 nights dinner, b & b) £165 for two, inclusive.

Examples from menus (revised seasonally, plus daily table d'hote): *lightly baked strips of avocado in curry sauce with mushrooms (in filo pastry), Cromer crab baked with fresh cream & asparagus tips; Dover sole stuffed with Norwegian prawns (breadcrumbed & deepfried), whole roast partridge fanned with apples & served with port wine sauce, sirloin steak Bordelaise, vegetarian cheese lasagne. Chocolate fetishists fondue, tropical fruit tartlet in mango & kiwi fruit sauce.*

In probably the best position in Felixstowe, this dignified Victorian edifice commands magnificent views over the sea and ferries, and the town centre is just to the rear. Now part of the well reputed Minotel Consortium, the Waverley has undergone extensive refurbishment, and the individual bedrooms each have first class amenities, some have balconies. The elegant Wolsey Restaurant draws on fresh produce from market garden and butchery. Likewise the opulent Gladstone Bar & Brasserie, where is served anything from a three course 'extravaganza' to a simple snack. Excellent facilities for conferences, business meetings, weddings and private functions.

THE RIVERSIDE THEATRE

Quayside, Woodbridge.

Tickets: Adults £3, children £2, students & OAP's £2.50.

Nestled on the shores of the river Deben in Woodbridge you will find the complex of the Riverside Restaurant and Theatre, where you can watch a top quality film in truly luxurious surrounds, drenched in the elegance of a bygone era. Its crystal chandaliers and tasteful rococo ceiling are enhanced by Wedgwood blue decor, generating a spacious, sumptuous and restful ambience. The sound is the latest Dolby stereo and the atmosphere is ofcourse smokeless. Besides films, the theatre is used for live shows and concerts, and can be hired for private functions, conferences and product launches.

THE RIVERSIDE RESTAURANT

Quayside, Woodbridge. Tel. (0394) 382587

Hours: Coffee 10 to 12 noon, lunch 12 to 3pm, Dinner 6 to 10:30pm, 7 days. Bar open all day.

Credit cards: Access, Visa.

Price guide: A la carte £15 – £20. Lunch £8.50 & £10.50 (2 & 3 courses).

Examples from a la carte (revised seasonally): *breast of wood pigeon in puff pastry with duxelles & port wine sauce, paupiette of sole with venison napped with a truffle cream; collops of monkfish poached with lime & ginger (garnished with mange tout), roast crispy duck with plum & brandy sauce (for 2), fillet of pork flamed in brandy & finished with cider stilton sauce, filo pastry parcels of ratatouille (set on a wine, cream & sorrell sauce. Homemade puddings.*

Once you have tasted the culinary delights of chefs Julian Robinson and Kevin Franklin at this air conditioned, garden-style restaurant, you will understand why its clientele is attracted from such a wide area! An extremely popular 'package' of amazing value is available – a night out for just £15, comprising a three-course dinner and theatre ticket. One can sip an aperitif or order a snack at the al fresco seating under a continental style canopy, or pop into the icecream parlour and spoil oneself with one (or more) of the 17 wondeful Italian flavours. The success of the complex is due to the hard work of the energetic young proprietor, Stuart Saunders, whose enthusiasm and attention to detail commands such a high standard – no surprise when you know that his brother, Steven, is proprietor of the celebrated Pink Geranium in Melbourn.

SECKFORD HALL

Near Woodbridge (off A12). Tel. (0394) 385678

Hours: 12:30 to 2pm, 7:30 to 9:30pm, 7 days. New Buttery from 10am to 10pm, except Mondays.
Credit cards: Access, Visa, Diners, Amex.
Price guide: A la carte £20. Table d'hote £11.50.
Accommodation: 34 rooms, all with private facilities, from £72 single, £85 double, inclusive. Some four-posters. 10 new luxury suites from £98 to £125.

Examples from menus (revised summer/winter, table d'hote daily, plus specials in the evenings): *North Sea sprats, mushroom & spinach mille feuille, crab au gratin, duck in a pancake; fresh lobster, sole & prawn pie, escalope of local venison, breast of goose with a chestnut & Grand Marnier sauce, noisetes of lamb in filo pastry, poached chicken on a mango & cointreau coulis, roast Gressingham duckling prepared with variety of sauces, hazelnut roast. Homemade sweets.*

Elizabeth Tudor once held court here, and it is certainly one of the region's most majestic and beautiful houses, surrounded by 34 acres of woodland and pasture, and overlooking a delightful trout lake. It's still fit for royalty, but one never feels overwhelmed, for the splendid interior is on a human scale, warm and hospitable. Furnishings are mostly period pieces, set against magnificent panelling, great oak doors and beams, and huge stone fireplaces. Modern comforts include an indoor pool, solarium gym and whirlpool, added by proprietor Michael Bunn, in whose family the Hall has been since 1950. Chef John Heeley favours fresh local produce, his speciality being lobster, kept live in a tank. More informal is the new Buttery, where the emphasis is on vegetarian and interesting light meals. Wonderful venue for wedding receptions, conferences etc.

THE OLD RECTORY

Campsea Ashe, near Woodbridge Tel. (0728) 746524

Hours: 7:30 to 9pm, Mon. – Sat. (except residents).
Credit cards: Access, Visa, Diners, Amex.
Price guide: £18.50 set price for four courses.
Accommodation: 6 doubles/twins en suite. £30 single, £50 double, inclusive.

Examples from menus (changed daily): *fresh scallops in reduction of tomato, onion & basil, wrapped in lettuce leaves and steamed; whole baked poussin stuffed beneath the skin with cream cheese, chutney & spices; delicate tart filled with seasonal fruit with a crunchy sesame seed topping.*

This handsome 17th century former rectory has appeared in most of the major guides in the eight years since Stewart Bassett came here. The gracious interior lives up to all expectations, with great open fireplaces and period furniture. The set four course menu is unashamedly limited (but changed daily), so one is assured of prime freshness, and many of the vegetables are local grown. The astonishing wine list of over 350 bins is one of the very largest in the region. Guests like to dine in the bright conservatory, with views over the lawned gardens, but there is also a private dining room. An ideal setting for private dinner parties and receptions, the Rectory is also well situated for the coast, golf courses, bird reserves and Snape Maltings, and makes an excellent place to stay.

THE SWAN HOTEL

Market Place, Southwold. Tel. (0502) 722186
Fax (0502) 724800

Hours: 12:15 to 1:45pm, 7:30 to 9:30pm, 7 days.
Credit cards: Access, Visa, Amex.
Price guide: 3 daily set menus (may be mixed), dinner £15.95, £19.95, £25. Lunch £9.75, £13.75, £16.50, £18.50.
Accommodation: 6 singles (from £38), 37 doubles/twins (from £75), 2 suites (from £115). Midweek winter breaks from £47 pp incl. dinner.

Examples from menus (changed daily): *smoked salmon & trout roulade with lemon mayonnaise, Southwold seafood sausage in a spaghetti of vegetables, warm brioche filled with foie gras served with port wine jelly; supreme of Henham duck carved onto an island of Claret sauce, breast of local pigeon grilled & placed around a woodland mushroom sauce, Welsh leg of lamb filled with chicken & basil mousse served on bed of red wine sauce, rib eye of Scottish steak braised with button onions & port wine, assiette of Suffolk cod & Sole Bay longshore fish bound in tarragon & white wine sauce, prime cuts of turbot steamed & served with tiger prawns & ginger sauce, lattice of salmon & brill on champagne sauce. Old English Suffolk curd tart with clotted cream, pancakes filled with cream & topped with chocolate fudge sauce, exotic fresh fruit terrine served with mango & strawberry sauce, chocolate cup (filled with cream cheese, kirsch & raspberries).*

Southwold is one of England's last unspoilt coastal towns, an enchanting throw-back to an age long past. At its heart is this classic 17th century hotel, remodelled in the 1820's, and the period refinement and elegance has not been lost to more recent modernisations. Like all the public rooms, the dining room is beautifully furnished, and serves as well for a function as a private dinner for two. The smaller informal Trellis Room, overlooking a tiny courtyard, is used as an extension or for private parties. Three fixed price menus offer a very considerable choice ranging from English classics to some highly original eclectic suggestions from the chef. He very much favours fresh seasonal produce, using home grown herbs and own-baked bread. Simpler fare is available in the bar, accompanied by an award winning Adnams ale, or perhaps a wine from the celebrated Adnams range. Afternoon teas are another timeless tradition well observed. Bedrooms are very well appointed, individually decorated, and have colour televisions, direct telephones and hair-dryers. Whilst every latest facility is there, the management takes pride in the fact that the hotel does not have vast, impersonal conference halls. The airy Reading Room, for example, can seat up to 50, fully equipped and with the option of secretarial services. There can be few more agreeable or tranquil places to do business, with the prospect of a brisk walk along the seashore followed by an excellent lunch or dinner. The world famous Aldeburgh Festival is held in June, not far down the 'Heritage Coast', but this is a lovely area to visit any time of the year.

Swan Hotel, Southwold.

THE CROWN HOTEL

High Street, Southwold. Tel. (0502) 722275

Hours: 12:30 to 2pm, 7:30 to 9:30pm, 7 days.
Credit cards: Access, Visa, Amex.
Price guide: Set price £15.50 (2 courses), £17.75 (3 courses). Lunch £12.75 (2 courses), £14.75 (3 courses). Bar meals from £1.75 – £8.50.
Accommodation: 2 singles (£33), 9 doubles/twins (£52), 1 family (£75), all with private facilities.

Examples from restaurant menus (changed daily): *fresh crab baked in filo pastry with herb sauce, gratin of spiced vegetables Malay; steamed fillet of turbot with watercress beurre fondue, medley of five fish with saffron sauce, magret of duck with piquant sauce, hot vegetarian quiche with tomato & basil sauce. Hot Bakewell tart with cream, lemon bavarois with fruit coulis. Bar: mussels with fennel sauce, vegetable curry, American fish chowder, haddock & prawn bake, spring chicken with apple & calvados sauce.*

Feted regularly by national newspapers and major food guides, The Crown enjoys a celebrity well beyond the region. Managed by Anne Simpson, it is a flagship for owners Adnams, whose brewery is near, and whose award-winning range of ales is available in both contrasting bars. Being also an esteemed wine merchant, the wine list is ofcourse exceptional, with nearly 300 vintages, many available by the glass. But it is as much the food, prepared by chef Andrew Mulliss and staff, which wins the plaudits. Its popularity means that booking in the restaurant is always advisable. The essence of an 18th century coaching inn is till much in evidence – antique furniture, old paintings and carved fireplaces – and the individual bedrooms are simple but attractive. Hotel closed one week in January.

THE DOVE RESTAURANT

Wortwell, Harleston (on A143 by-pass) Tel. (098 686) 315

Hours: Anytime, but booking required.
Credit cards: Access, Visa.
Price guide: A la carte £12 to £20, Sun. lunch £8.50.
Accommodation: 3 doubles/twins (2 en suite), £30 dble, £17.50 sngle, B & B.

Examples from menus (revised seasonally): *seafood pancake, melon with curried prawns, own recipe venison pie, ragout fruits de mer, scampi Provencal, coquilles St. Jacques, chicken supreme, own recipe steak and kidney pie, trout, steaks. Crepe maison (pancake filled with raspberries, or orange or lemon, and pastry cream), meringue Chantilly, syllabub, chocolate eclair.*

Simple, country restaurants serving honest home cooked food are among the best reasons for visiting France. However, one need only travel as far as the A 143 by pass near Wortwell to experience the same pleasure. Chef Patron John Oberhoffer, recipient of the Cordon Culinaire award and the Association Culinaire Francais de Londres winner's medal, is a distinguished practioner of the art of French country cooking. With wife Pat he has over the last 12 years established the Dove as a much admired restaurant, not just for good food but for the unpretentious manner in which it is presented, and at very reasonable prices. They are pleased to cater for private parties up to 30, and also offer a good breakfast after a comfortable night in one of the refurbished bedrooms – you are well placed here in the lovely Waveney Valley for business or pleasure. A 'Dove' has stood on this acre of ground, bordering a stream, since around the time of the French Revolution.

WEAVERS WINE BAR & RESTAURANT

Market Hill, Diss

Hours: Mon. – Fri. 12 to 2pm, Mon .– Sat. 7 to 9:30pm. Not Christmas.
Credit cards: Access, Visa.
Price guide: A la carte £15. Lunch £7.50 (three courses).

Examples from menus (revised weekly): *timballe of smoked salmon filled with lobster mousse, chicken liver & smoked bacon pate; collops of roast loin of venison (set over a creme de cassis, blackcurrant & Dijon mustard sauce), whole lemon sole panfried in parsley butter & lemon juice, homebaked steak kidney & mushroom pie topped with flaky pastry. Lunch: seafood tagliatelle, lightly poached breast of pigeon in whole grain mustard. Hot squidgy coffee & walnut sponge.*

The prosperous Weavers' Guild built this as a chapel in the 15th century. The solemnity and formality of their religion is in little evidence today, however, for now it is a bright, relaxed and very popular wine bar cum restaurant, with a fast growing reputation. This has been the achievement of chef/proprietor William Bavin and wife Wilma, who refurbished the building, exposing and treating the ancient timbers, and opened for business in April '87. From the simple wooden tables, with a little vase of flowers on each, diners can view the narrow streets of this pleasant little town through enormous windows. The lunch menu, like the dinner menu always unusual and interesting, is chalked on a daily blackboard, accompanied perhaps by a good French country wine, and maybe one of the excellent range of malt whiskies. Besides being very reasonably priced, the food is fresh, and herbs are grown in the courtyard for use in the kitchen.

SALISBURY HOUSE RESTAURANT WITH ROOMS

Victoria Road, Diss. Tel. (0379) 644738

Hours: 12:15 to 1:45pm, Tues. – Fri. 7:30 to 9:15pm, Tues. – Sat.
Credit cards: Access, Visa.
Price guide: A la carte from £20. Lunch (by appointment) from £11.50.
Accommodation: 3 en suite bedrooms (1 with whirlpool bath), from £54 per room, £36 single. One 4-poster bedroom in separate annex.

Examples from menus (revised monthly): *chicken & brie mousseline with creamy chablis sauce, roast loin of hare with wild mushrooms on seasonal leaf salad, stilton pear & white port pate with toasted brioche; salmon with scallop mousseline & Noilly Prat & saffron sauce, brace of boneless quails filled with red pepper mousse served with muscat grape sauce, fillet of lamb with fresh basil & tomato sauce. Mousse of white Belgian chocolate with coffee bean sauce, pine kernel tart with blackcurrant sauce, poppy seed parfait with ragout of dates.*

Set well back from the main road, surrounded by an acre of mature gardens, this tranquil and gracious old house is much older than it looks, for it was originally built as a store for the nearby windmill, and only the facade is Victorian. Proprietors Barry and Sue Davies have furnished in keeping with the spirit of a relaxing country home, and added a beautiful conservatory where (when it's warm!) diners may gaze out over the splendid floodlit gardens. They may prefer to concentrate on Barry's excellent cooking, which has secured a place in just about every major food guide. A quite extraordinary wine list numbers over 200, with a particularly good range of clarets and half bottles. Very comfortable accommodation, and reasonably priced. Private meetings/functions welcome – marquee if appropriate.

MARCO'S

17 Pottergate, Norwich. Tel. (0603) 624044

Hours: 12:30 to 2pm, 7:30 to 10pm, Tues. – Sat.
Credit cards: Access, Visa, Diners, Amex.
Price guide: A la carte £24. Lunch £16.

Examples from menus (revised weekly): *Marco's potato gnocchi, tagliatelli verdi alla gorgonzola, Norfolk crab salad with avocado pear & mango sauce; buridda alla Genovese (fish stew), scampi allo spumante (sauted with chopped onion, mushrooms, asti spumante, fresh cream & almonds), breast of chicken (sauted with king prawns, onions, sweet peppers, fresh ginger, herbs, white wine & tomato sauce). Homemade icecreams/sorbets, fresh fruit baked in paper parcel with strawberry sauce.*

Royalty, film stars and other notables have dined here, but the food is just as good and the welcome as warm for we humbler mortals. In fact, Marco derives particular satisfaction from entertaining the grown up children of his early customers – his last 21 years have been given to making this one of the region's most respected restaurants, and a regular in all the main guides, with the philosophy that all food is good, and should be treated with care but without pretensions. Although an anglophile, he is dismayed that some customers still think Italians eat only pasta and pizzas! Guests may enter the kitchen at any time, and will notice part of a medieval wall, and a Victorian oven in which bread is baked. The Chinese influence in the bar seems incongruous at first, until you remember Marco Polo, and the small dining room is elegant, in keeping with this 17th century house. Outstanding Italian wine list.

BRASTED'S

8–10 St. Andrews Hill, Norwich Tel. (0603) 625949 Fax (0603) 766445

Hours: Mon. – Fri. 12 to 2pm and 7 to 10pm. Sat. 7 to 10pm.

Credit cards: Access, Visa, Diners, Amex.

Price guide: A la carte £19.

Examples from menus (revised seasonally): *ragout of seafood, leek and asparagus mousse (served warm with lemon and chervil sauce), steak tartare Caucasien, salad du canard; lamb en croute, medallions of pork in wild mushroom sauce, roast quail, rabbit pie, fillets of sole John Brasted (with mixture of fresh crabmeat, finished with prawn and saffron sauce), saumon en paupiette. Desserts and savoury finishes.*

In the city centre, just "a stone's throw" from the cathedral and castle, Brasteds nestles in a quiet cobbled street surrounded by history and next to the ancient Bridewell prison, now a museum. The menu offers a combination of classic English and sophisticated European dishes, and the care with which they are prepared by chef Paul Chipperfield is apparent from the beautiful presentation. But first take drinks in the homely morning room, then into the dining room, quite unique with its draped walls and ceilings creating the illusion of a tent. Combined with the polished wood floor and Persian rugs, the effect is warm and comfortable. First class service is always evident, and if you're lucky so is John Brasted himself! He is particularly proud of the quality local fish prominent on the menu, and it is refreshing to find savoury finishes as well as mouthwatering desserts. A balanced and comprehensive wine list includes a selection of very fine old wines (not exorbitant!), and an 1878 fine champagne by Bellairs is a distinguished cognac from a good choice.

ADLARD'S

79 Upper St. Giles Street, Norwich. Tel.(0603) 633522

Hours: 12:30 to 1:45pm, Tues. – Fri. 7:30 to 9pm, Tues. – Sat.

Credit cards: Access, Visa.

Price guide: Set price £27 (3 courses), £29 (4 courses).
Lunch £15 (2 courses), £17 (3 courses).

Examples from menus (revised daily): *seized scallops with spinach & sauce perfumed with citrus fruits, Norfolk asparagus with fresh crisp vermicelli (tossed in virgin olive oil with parmesan, tarragon & tomato coulis); fricassee of seafood a la nage (with lobster fumet & dill with basmati & wild rice), breast of Gressingham duck (with confit of duck, julienne of vegetables garlic & ginger wrapped in Chinese pancake, gratin dauphinois; green salad or cheese; parfait of two chocolates with mint creme anglaise, tulip of caramel icecream with roasted pears.*

One of a very select band of English restaurants to be awarded a rare Michelin star, and an Egon Ronay rosette, makes this one of the region's elite – the accomplishment of David and Mary Adlard, who moved from Wymondham three years ago to this 18th century grade II listed building, in a pleasant cul-de-sac near the R.C. cathedral. David learned his craft at The Connaught, London, is known as a perfectionist, and appeared on national tv recently, but for all the formidable reputation there is no pretentiousness; simple polished beech flooring on three tiers is nicely complemented by striking green wall fabric and original oil paintings, and the atmosphere is relaxed and unstarchy. Exceptional wine list of 150 bins from all over the world.

THE NORFOLK MEAD HOTEL

Coltishall, nr Norwich. Tel. (0603) 737531

Hours: 7 to 9pm Mon – Sat, 12 to 2pm Sun.
Credit cards: Access, Visa, Diners, Amex.
Price guide: Fixed price a la carte £15.95 and £21.50.
Accommodation: 10 doubles/twins, all en suite, 1 with '2-berth' jacuzzi, 1 with 4-poster. From £45 single, £60 double. Weekly half board from £265, weekend breaks from £77.

Examples from menus (revised seasonally): *pan-fried slice of sweetbread terrine on bed of carrot spaghetti, warm salad of seafood asparagus & pasta; steamed fillet of salmon with tomatoes & basil on butter sauce, boned saddle of rabbit with lemon & thyme stuffing, grilled breast of duck on sharp lime sauce, avocado stuffed with cream cheese & walnuts baked in golden puff pastry. Baked filo pastry of pineapple & mango with white chocolate & malibu icecream, hot pear clafoutis, fondant tomatoes on toast topped with gruyere cheese.*

The country house hotel is a cherished English institution, and here is as fine an example as one could hope for, near The Broads, Blickling Hall and Norwich. An 18th century manor house, it stands in 12 lovely acres sloping gently to a long river frontage – one can arrive by boat, car or helicopter! Beautifully restored by proprietors Reg Davies and Jane Seymour, it affords every comfort, indeed luxury, but with no hint of stuffiness. One can lounge in the heated pool in the walled garden in summer, or get just as wet hiring a rowboat on the river, and there is a fishing lake in the grounds. The restaurant and chef Chris Hyde enjoy a first class reputation for interesting dishes superbly presented.

KNAPTON HALL HOTEL

The Street, Knapton, nr North Walsham.

Tel. (0263) 720405
Fax (0263) 721692

Hours:	12 to 2pm, 7:30 to 10pm, 7 days, restaurant & bar.
Credit cards:	Access, Visa, Amex.
Price guide:	A la carte from £15. Bar snacks from £2.
Accommodation:	6 doubles, 1 single, 2 twins, all with private facilities.

Examples from menus (revised monthly): *poached fillet of salmon with light natural yoghurt & fresh mint dressing. baked sea bass with Pernod & fennel cream sauce, fillet steak Knapton Hall (stuffed with king prawns & glazed with stilton. Sticky toffee pudding with butterscotch sauce, peach & orange roulade, savouries.*

This striking Georgian oddity looks as though it has been lifted from the stockbroker belt and dropped in the midst of flint cottages and farmland. The gentleman who built it as his country home obviously had taste, however. Apart from the two acres of landscaped gardens, the interior is elegant and well proportioned. Modern amenity is not lacking; the rooms have been fully refurbished and there is an indoor pool and sauna. In the superb dining room the aptly named new chef, Phillip Hill, presents classic French cuisine – to keep abreast of changes ask to be on the monthly mailing list. Wines range from the simple to the classics, with clarets well represented, being a 'hobby' of the proprietor. Sunday lunch is particularly noted, served from an unusual copperdome trolley. Well placed for Norwich and coast. Egon Ronay rated.

GREEN FARM RESTAURANT & HOTEL

North Walsham Road, Thorpe Market. Tel. (0263) 833602

Hours: 7 to 9:30pm (10pm Fri & Sat) every evening, Sun lunch. Weekday lunches by arrangement. Bar open lunch & evening every day.

Credit cards: Access, Visa.

Price guide: A la carte £20, chef's supper £16.25.

Accommodation: 6 doubles (from £35), 1 single (from £41.50), all en suite. 2 with 4-posters. Some with facilities for disabled. Tourist Board 4 Crowns. Special breaks.

Examples from menus (revised every 8 – 10 weeks): *smoked salmon roulade with avocado mousse, savoury pear with tarragon cream dressing; lemon sorbet; roast poussin with celery & lemon stuffing & sultana & redcurrant sauce, fresh daily fish, sirloin steak with Drambuie & wild mushrooms, pasta & mushrooms baked with mozarella & stilton. Bar meals: baked mushrooms & walnut topping, deep fried brie with redcurrant sauce, salads of Lord Suffield's spiced beef & Edward VII salmon. Trad Sun roast £5.50.*

This tranquil little backwater, flint cottages huddled round a small village green, is an ideal retreat from urban pressures. One is cosseted in every creature comfort; each bedroom has a style its own, furnished with antiques yet lacking no modern convenience; fresh flowers, fruit and homemade chocolates replenished daily; and a restaurant recognised as one of the area's best. Chef proprietor Philip Lomax prepares many of his own, unique dishes, a delight to eye and palate. There's so much to see in these parts: Felbrigg and Blickling Halls are not far, neither is the lovely coast, nor the fine city of Norwich, nor the Broads. Recommended by most major good food and hotel guides.

THE MIRABELLE

Station Road, West Runton, Cromer. Tel. (0263) 75396

Hours: . Open for lunch & dinner (last orders 9:15pm). Closed Mondays. Closed Sunday evenings in winter.

Credit cards: Access, Visa, Diners, Amex.

Price guide: A la carte £16 – £20. Table d'hote £16.50 – £19. Lunch £11.

Examples from menus (a la carte revised seasonally, table d'hote daily): *aubergine Viennoise, fresh asparagus with artichoke & smoked salmon, sauted kidneys on toast; poached salmon with lobster sauce, grilled skate with capers & burnt butter, roast Norfolk duckling with apple sauce, sauted beef with tarragon & cream, Wienerschnitzel, jugged hare with redcurrant jelly & spatzil, chicken Viennoise. Souffle glace Grand Marnier, creme brulee.*

A truly awesome wine list of over 350 is one of the largest in the country, yet one would never guess that such a distinguished restaurant – quite an institution here in North Norfolk – lies behind such a modest (though not unattractive) frontage. One steps into a large, bustling French restaurant, but the proprietor, Manfred Hollwoger, is Austrian. Two set price menus and an a la carte add up to en extensive choice (including some Germanic alternatives), with local seafood and game the house specialities, and vegetarians are not forgotten. Look out for gourmet nights in winter, and do try to book ahead in summer and for weekends at any time, for this is one of the most popular restaurants in the area.

THE ARK

The Street, Erpingham, nr. Cromer Tel. (0263) 761535

Hours: 7 to 9:30pm Tues – Sat (Nov. to Easter Wed – Sat). 12:30 to 2pm, Wed – Sat.
Credit cards: not accepted
Price guide: A la carte £14 – £17. Special suppers Tues – Thurs £11. Lunch £10 – £12.
Accommodation: 2 en suite rooms, 1 with direct access to garden.

Examples from menus (revised daily and according to season):*aubergine tri hors d'oeuvre, crab & mango salad, herb cheese pate with tomato & orange; "weeping" lamb with potatoes & mushroom gratin, grilled mackerel with gooseberry sauce, lobster, spinach & ricotta pancakes. Apple quince & ginger suet pud, chocolate mousse with coffee sauce, Mrs Beton's lemon & almond tart.*

English visitors to France are beguiled by the family-run country restaurants serving good, wholesome food at reasonable prices, and lament their rarity in England. Well, here is just such a one, in an exquisite flint cottage a little off the beaten track from Norwich to Cromer, now with the extra bonus of overnight accommodation. One feels very much a personal guest of owners Mike and Sheila Kidd (daughter Becky assists in the kitchen); the dining room is homely and informal, and from here one can rest the eyes on the two acre garden, where herbs and vegetables are grown and picked daily for the kitchen, absolutely fresh, particularly important in the vegetarian dish always featured. All is prepared on the premises, including bread and chocolates, and even jams, pickles and curds. Recommended by major good food guides.

THE 'GAMP' RESTAURANT

Claypit Lane, Foulsham, E. Dereham. Tel. (036 284) 4114

Hours: Lunch & dinner, Tues. – Sat. Monday evening by appointment. Trad. Sun. lunch.

Credit cards: Access, Visa, Mastercard, Eurocard.

Price guide: A la carte £16, lunch £9.95 (both incl. service). Wednesday night special: 12ozs rump steak or duck £6.

Examples from menus (revised 6-weekly): *Swiss rosti with Cumberland sausage, fricassee of seafood finished with dry vermouth sauce; crisp roast Norfolk duckling with rich bittersweet pink grapefruit sauce, puff pastry parcel of monkfish with mushroom & fennel on mushroom sauce, dry fried beef fillet caramelised with Dijon mustard & finished in brandy & shallot sauce, vegetable ragout, grills. Dark rich chocolate & Cointreau cream served with macaroon biscuits, apple & rhubarb tart served warm with chantilly cream.*

A 'gamp' is an umbrella, which is how one landlord 'repaired' his tenant's leaky roof in the early 1900s. The name stuck, and owners (for over a year) Andy and Daphne Bush are not about to change it. The only 'leeks' these days are prepared in the kitchen, for their first task was to restore and enhance their charming 200-year-old cottage. Andy trained at Westminster College and Connaught Hotel, and takes pride in presenting wholesome, tasty dishes from fresh local produce, with a hint of French classical style. One may request alternative healthier ingredients to enjoy with a clear conscience – hours are flexible, too. Although always good value, at only £6 the Wednesday night special is extraordinarily so. The 45-bin wine list draws from 15 countries, and includes some classics. An outstanding collection of Norfolk landscape photographs (for sale) adorn the two very pleasant dining rooms.

GREY GABLES COUNTRY HOUSE HOTEL & RESTAURANT

Norwich Road, Cawston. Tel. (0603) 871259

Hours: Dinner 7 days (last orders 8:30 – 9pm). Lunch by arrangement.
Credit cards: Access, Visa.
Price guide: Set price £16, £18, £20, for 3, 4, & 5 courses.
Accommodation: From £42 pp single, £24 pp double. Two night special breaks (dinner, bed & breakfast) from £58 pp.

Examples from menus (revised weekly): *mussels in cream sauce, Norfolk ham with redcurrant jelly & peas pudding; plum sorbet, yellow pea soup, smoked salmon; roast rib of beef served with spicy mustard sauce, pheasant cooked with celery apple wine & cream sauce, local plaice with almonds, stilton parcel roasted in puff pastry. Three desserts to try at table, cheeses. Coffee & petits fours included.*

With so many anonymous plastic motels springing up at our roadsides, it is reassuring that such quiet country houses still thrive, personally supervised by the proprietors. This 18th century rectory is a perfect retreat, hidden by tall trees in a leafy lane just a few miles from Norwich. One is made to feel more like a personal guest than a paying customer; James Snaith invites arrivals into the lounge for drinks, then into the warm and homely candlelit dining room to enjoy Rosalind's unpretentious home cooking, always using fresh, wholesome ingredients. The awful dilemma of choosing a sweet is simply dispensed with – you have all three! James, an aficianado of good wines, stocks an amazing 200 plus, including many classics. Business people should consider holding small meetings here; it's quiet, and there's the prospect of an excellent lunch! Special two days (or more) breaks are good value.

SHIPDHAM PLACE HOTEL & RESTAURANT

Church Close, Shipdham, nr E. Dereham. Tel. (0362) 820303

Hours: Open every day for morning coffee, afternoon tea & dinner, lunch by arrangement.
Credit cards: Access, Visa.
Price guide: Table d'hote £18.50 (3 courses), £23.50 (5 courses).
Accommodation: 8 doubles/twins, all with private facilities, 2 with 4-posters. From £30 single, £40 double.

Examples from menus (changed daily): *chicken terrine with plum coulis, scallop in puff pastry, crab claws with herb mayonnaise, halibut steaks poached in yoghurt with a hollandaise, veal tournedos with cream & chive sauce, duck breasts with herb butter, fillet beef woith mustard sauce. Fruit & chocolate shortbread, brandy cream, plums in red wine, chestnut & honey icecream.*

East Anglia is noted for its wealth of medieval churches, but adjacent are quite often found beautiful and graceful old rectories. Shipdham Place ranks amongst the best. Its rooms tell of a more elegant and dignified age than our own – just what most of us look for as a place to stay when travelling on business or pleasure. One is in the very heart of Norfolk here, and the commodious rooms are reasonably priced. Almost as a bonus, the restaurant is also of the first order, well worth a visit even if you are not staying. Proprietors Alan and Tina Poulton (who cooks) offer daily set menus of four or five dishes per course. Great emphasis is placed on freshness – most of the herbs and vegetables have only to travel the short distance from the garden. Interesting wine list.

THE GRANARY HOTEL & RESTAURANT

Little Dunham, nr Swaffham. Tel. (0328) 701310

Hours:	Lunch & evening every day, afternoon teas.
Credit cards:	Access, Visa, Diners, Amex.
Price guide:	A la carte £15, lunch from £11. Sun lunch £9.95.
Accommodation:	2 doubles, 8 twins, 3 family, all with full facilities. £35 single, £45 double.

Examples from menu (revised quarterly): *tiger tails (prawns) in garlic & herbs, chef's chicken liver pate blended with cognac & cream; tournedos Arizona (fillet steak filled with stilton, wrapped in bacon, with madeira sauce), seafood crepinette (wholewheat pancake filled with shellfish, topped with asparagus & glazed with cheese), Breckland duckling in rich berry sauce laced with cherry brandy, vegetarian wholewheat pancake. Homemade puddings. Bar snacks.*

Ashley Courtenay recommends this as one of the most unusual hotels visited. Cleverly converted from 18th century barns by farmer-proprietors Mr and Mrs Jim Harris, it is set on three sides of a square (with central garden), the fourth open to permit views over the lake (fishing) and golf course. Sturdy old beams, polished wood floors and brick walls combine most felicitously, and there's a magnificent open fireplace in the restaurant. Chef George Crummett presents English and continental cuisine, using home produced vegetables and meat from the farm whenever possible. Besides golf and fishing there's a grass tennis court, outdoor heated pool, table tennis, and riding and shooting by arrangement. Well placed for Sandringham, Castle Acre and many other local attractions. Bedrooms clean and comfortable. Facilities for disabled and pets. Well behaved children welcome.

FISHES

Market Place, Burnham Market. Tel. (0328) 738588

Hours: Lunch & dinner (last orders 9:30pm, 9pm in winter) Tues. – Sun. Closed over Christmas and two weeks in January.

Credit cards: Access, Visa, Diners, Amex.

Price guide: A la carte £14. Lunch £6.50 (2 courses), £7.75 (3 courses). Sunday lunch £7.45 (2 courses), £8.95 (3 courses).

Examples from menus (a la carte revised seasonally, lunches daily): *oysters, smoked eel, lobster, Brancaster mussels, gravlax; home baked ham and smoked goose breast, halibut with garlic butter, wild Scottish salmon, river trout with almonds and bananas, monkfish with parsley & Mussel sauce, salmon fishcakes with crab sauce, salad of tomato leek and black olives, salad of dates oranges and nuts. Syllabub, fresh date cheesecake, meringues with kiwi fruit, West Indian gateau.*

Nelson was born very near and probably spent some damp childhood days in the stream which runs right past the door of 'Fishes'. Burnham Market is a very picturesque, unspoilt village, among the best in Norfolk. It is well placed to receive Neptune's bounty – shrimps from Wells, oysters from Burnham Norton, the cleanest mussels in the land from Brancaster, the famous crabs and lobster from Cromer, and seafish from Lowestoft. Vegetables come fresh from local market gardeners. Fishes receives regular plaudits from prestigious national guides, but is cheerfully unpretentious, decked out bistro style with cork tables and floors, and in summer the window is full of 'Morning Glories'. The cold display looks tempting, and lobsters are kept live in a tank out of view. Childrens' portions available.

CONGHAM HALL COUNTRY HOUSE HOTEL

Grimston, near Kings Lynn. Tel. (0485) 600250

Hours: Lunch and dinner (last orders 9:30pm). Closed Sat. lunchtime
Credit cards: Access, Visa, Diners, Amex.
Price guide: A la carte £30, lunch £15.
Accommodation: 14 rooms (all en suite), from £70 single, £105 double.

Examples from menus (revised seasonally): *chilled mousseline of salmon & scallops encased by local lobster (on vegetable & caviar dressing), warm terrine of goats cheese & potato & spinach (on balsamic vinaigrette, with walnut bread); Norfolk crab bisque; pan fried fillet of beef wrapped in garden herbs with truffle cream & chateaubriand sauces, escallope of turbot braised in champagne, steamed heart of artichoke finished with vegetable ragout on tomato pasta with riesling sauce. Chilled coffee & rum terrine layered with marzipan & pistachio icecream on patterned sauce, variety of cheese fritters on tomato basil sauce.*

The RAC blue ribbon, AA rosette and red star are not casually awarded, but Congham Hall has them all, a rare achievement for proprietors Trevor and Christine Forecast, who supervise personally. A member of the exclusive 'Pride of Britain' consortium, theirs is surely one of the most prestigious country hotels in the region, to be found in all the best food and hotel guides. It is also among the region's most beautiful houses, a Georgian Manor set in 40 acres of lovely parkland and gardens, including a large kitchen herb garden, open to the public at certain times. Chef Clive Jackson favours fresh local produce in creating his classic English and French dishes, and has a flair for presentation.

GARBO'S RESTAURANT

7 Saturday Market Place, Kings Lynn   Tel. (0553) 773136

Hours: 7:30 to 10pm, Tues. – Sat. Please book.
Credit cards: Access, Visa.
Price guide: A la carte £15 – £20.

West Norfolk Newspapers Ltd

Examples from menus (revised twice weekly): *carrot & orange soup served with cream cheese scones, boned quail filled with marinated wild rabbit & pistachio nuts served with lentil & truffle vinaigrette, mousse of bloater wrapped in smoked sea trout served with dill & mustard sauce; fillet of lamb wrapped in tarragon mousse served with celeriac & sauce of madeira, layers of salmon & local mussels topped with puff pastry & served with sauce of vermouth & cream, aubergine layered with roast peppers & smoked cheddar & pine nuts served with white wine sauce. Gratin of orange with marmalade icecream in biscuit basket, dark chocolate marquise with coffee bean sauce, Garbo's style sherry syllabub trifle.*

The Guardian and Independent newspapers recently ran favourable reviews of this relative newcomer to the Norfolk scene. The vegetarian good food guide awarded a star rating, and recognition has come from the Michelin guide – Chef patron Steve and partner Clair have put Kings Lynn on the gastronomic map. One could be forgiven for mistaking their friendly 32 seater restaurant for a wine bar cum bistro: the Hollywood theme (established by the many photographs of film stars), polished wood tables and informal atmosphere suggest it, but the imaginative menu clearly places it in another class. The style of cooking is best described as English with French and Italian influences. All is homemade, including sorbets, icecream, bread and chocolates, and the menu reflects availability of fresh local produce.

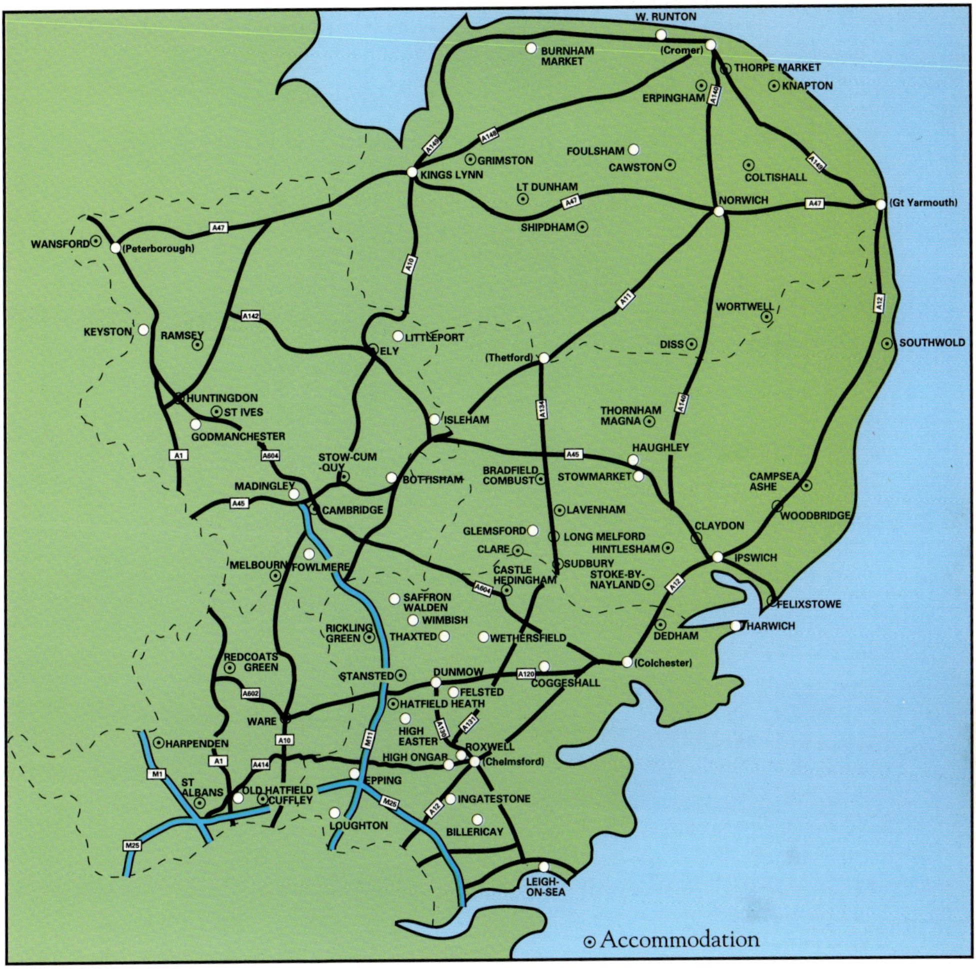

LOCATOR MAP
Eastern Counties

Index

CAMBRIDGESHIRE

ESSEX

HERTFORDSHIRE

Index

HERTFORDSHIRE *(continued)*

NORFOLK

SUFFOLK

* accommodation

ADNAMS
WINE MERCHANTS
"BRITAIN'S MOST INTERESTING WINE MERCHANT"
Recioto
Languedoc
...a region reborn
CALIFORNIA
CHATEAU CLIMENS
1er CRU
HAUT-BARSAC
BORDEAUX
1989 VINTAGE
ADNAMS
1991 WINE LIST
ADNAMS
1990 WINE LIST
BAILEYS
CLASSIC STYLE
SHIRAZ
PETALUMA
CHÂTEAU BEYCHEVELLE
ACHILLE-FOULD
Laurent-Perrier
THE CROWN, HIGH STREET, SOUTHWOLD, SUFFOLK IP18 6DP
TELEPHONE: SOUTHWOLD (0502) 724222 FAX: (0502) 724805
Regional Wine Merchant of the Year
SUNDAY TELEGRAPH/WINE MAGAZINE GOOD WINE GUIDE 1991